Cambridge Elements

Elements in Politics and Society in Southeast Asia
edited by
Edward Aspinall
Australian National University
Meredith L. Weiss
University at Albany, SUNY

THE POLITICS OF CROSS-BORDER MOBILITY IN SOUTHEAST ASIA

Michele Ford
The University of Sydney

Shaftesbury Road, Cambridge CB2 8EA, United Kingdom

One Liberty Plaza, 20th Floor, New York, NY 10006, USA

477 Williamstown Road, Port Melbourne, VIC 3207, Australia

314–321, 3rd Floor, Plot 3, Splendor Forum, Jasola District Centre, New Delhi – 110025, India

103 Penang Road, #05–06/07, Visioncrest Commercial, Singapore 238467

Cambridge University Press is part of Cambridge University Press & Assessment, a department of the University of Cambridge.

We share the University's mission to contribute to society through the pursuit of education, learning and research at the highest international levels of excellence.

www.cambridge.org
Information on this title: www.cambridge.org/9781009462426

DOI: 10.1017/9781108673914

First published 2023

A catalogue record for this publication is available from the British Library

ISBN 978-1-009-46242-6 Hardback
ISBN 978-1-108-72289-6 Paperback
ISSN 2515-2998 (online)
ISSN 2515-298X (print)

The Politics of Cross-border Mobility in Southeast Asia

Elements in Politics and Society in Southeast Asia

DOI: 10.1017/9781108673914
First published online: December 2023

Michele Ford
The University of Sydney

Author for correspondence: Michele Ford, michele.ford@sydney.edu.au

Abstract: This Element explains how cross-border mobility defines diplomatic relationships between Southeast Asian states and social and political dynamics within the region's key destination countries. It begins by providing a historically situated discussion of bordering processes within the region, examining evolving historical conceptions of power and sovereignty and processes of bordering in colonial and post-colonial times. It then turns to the political, environmental and economic drivers of contemporary cross-border mobility before examining governments' efforts to manage different kinds of border-crossers and the tensions that these efforts generate. Having discussed the politics of cross-border mobility in host communities, the Element returns to the question of why consideration of bordering practices and cross-border mobility is necessary in understanding contemporary Southeast Asia.

Keywords: refugees, asylum seekers, human trafficking, labour migration, bordering practices

ISBNs: 9781009462426 (HB), 9781108722896 (PB), 9781108673914 (OC)
ISSNs: 2515-2998 (online), 2515-298X (print)

Contents

1 Introduction

As a region, Southeast Asia is indelibly marked by centuries of mobility into and between the different geographical spaces that now comprise its contemporary states. The introduction of modern technologies like passports was preceded by extensive patterns of mobility across what have since become national borders, from the sea people (*orang laut*) of the Malay World to the upland tribes that inhabit the mountainous region traversing parts of Vietnam, Laos, Thailand and Myanmar. The legacies of these historic flows are evident in Southeast Asia's ethnic make-up, but also its architecture, languages, religious practices and cuisines. They have shaped trading relationships and the contours of the region's economic development, and fuelled social tensions, separatist conflicts and border disputes.

Cross-border mobility also contributes to the region's contemporary demographic structure. Migrants represent a much smaller proportion of the population in Asia than in Oceania, North America or Europe. However, the Asian region is the source of over 40 per cent of international migrants – some 111 million people – 66 million of whom live in another Asian country or in the Middle East. Many of these migrants are from Southeast Asia. In absolute terms, the Philippines and Indonesia are among the top twenty countries of origin for international migration, while Thailand and Malaysia are among the top twenty destination countries. As a proportion of its population, Singapore has one of the highest concentrations of migrants in the world. Myanmar, meanwhile, is a top-ten source country for refugees and is in the top four globally for stateless persons.

It is no accident, then, that cross-border mobility has such a strong influence on the region's political and social terrain. It is impossible to truly understand diplomatic relationships *between* Southeast Asian states without considering cross-border flows. As I argue in this Element, moreover, serious consideration of contemporary patterns of cross-border mobility is necessary if we are to understand social and political dynamics *within* the region's key destination countries for asylum seekers and economic migrants. Yet, beyond studies of borderlands, refugee flows, labour migration – and to some extent the scholarship on international relations – cross-border mobility barely registers with the vast majority of scholars of Southeast Asia.

This Element sets out the case for recognition of cross-border mobility as a defining feature of Southeast Asia. Section 2 provides an historically situated discussion of bordering processes within the region, examining evolving historical conceptions of power and sovereignty, and processes of bordering in colonial and post-colonial times. Section 3 then outlines the political, environmental and economic drivers of contemporary cross-border mobility, while Section 4 turns to governments' efforts to manage asylum seekers, temporary labour migrants and spontaneous economic migrants, and the tensions that arise in the process. The final section examines the politics of mobility in host communities, with a focus on processes of othering, the emergence of a foreign underclass and the fossilisation of gender norms. The Element concludes by returning to the question of why consideration of bordering practices and cross-border mobility is so necessary if we are to understand contemporary Southeast Asia.

2 Of Nations and Borders

Borders define modern nation-states in ways both physical and symbolic, acting as pivots between territorial states and transnational flows (van Schendel 2005). As border studies scholars argue, borders play an active role in the construction of the nation-state as markers of statehood, 'the political membranes through which people, goods, wealth, and information must pass' (Horstmann 2004, 8).

Many Southeast Asian borders are surrounded by dense economic and social webs that bind the communities they divide (Mahanty 2022). It is these webs, along with the different opportunity structures available on each side of a border, that encourage cross-border flows of people and goods (Horstmann and Wadley 2006). Of course, not all borders are equal: before the advent of the oil palm boom, isolated borderlands in the middle of the island of Borneo were barely visible to the Indonesian and Malaysian authorities. Many borders in the highlands of Mainland Southeast Asia remain invisible even today. By contrast, some borders within the region – most emblematically, the narrow straits between Singapore, Malaysia and Indonesia – are among the most closely surveilled borders in the world (Ford and Lyons 2013).

But even the most highly policed borders in the region are to some extent porous, as the Singapore example reveals. When I was conducting fieldwork in the mid-2000s in the Singapore-Indonesia borderlands, I met Jali in the Indonesian port town of Tanjung Pinang in the Riau Islands. Jali told me how he would drop loads of mangrove wood from at an unofficial port (*pelabuhan tikus,* lit. mouse port) at the mouth of a small stream in the Singapore district of Jurong before returning with second-hand goods, which he sold upon his return.[1] According to Jali, 'The Singaporean customs guys didn't care what we brought in, but Indonesian customs boats patrol the straits. The most that ever happened though is that they'd ask for one of the TVs.'

The experience of Mukyu, now the owner of a small furniture shop in Tanjung Pinang, attests to the porousness even of Singapore's official border

1 For a discussion of 'mouse ports' in the Riau Islands, see Ford and Lyons (2013).

posts. Although she did not have an import permit, or even an appropriate visa, Mukyu used to travel back and forth on a commercial ferry, bringing clothes from Indonesia to sell in Singapore. Indeed, it was only with the advent of COVID-19 that this particular border effectively closed when the commercial ferries plying the routes between the Indonesian islands of Bintan, Batam and Karimun ceased operations in response to border restrictions and declining income (Fadli 2020a, 2020b). Such stories of border-crossing – but also of states' attempts to control or prevent it – abound in contemporary Southeast Asia.

2.1 Conceptions of Sovereignty

Before reflecting on the contemporary nature of Southeast Asia's borderlands, it is helpful to take a step back and understand the history of contemporary national borders, and the processes through which those borders formed. Even more so, it is necessary to consider the precolonial conceptions of sovereignty displaced by them, and the insights that those conceptions provide into contemporary bordering practices.

Southeast Asia has long been an important focus for theorising alternatives to Westphalian models of sovereignty. Famously, Anderson (2007, 28) captured the concrete, embodied understanding of power found in classical Javanese thought by likening the traditional Javanese polity to 'a cone of light cast downwards by a reflector lamp', in which the power of one ruler merges 'imperceptibly with the ascending Power of a neighbouring sovereign'. This 'gradual, even diminution of the radiance of the lamp with increasing distance from the bulb', he argued, 'is an exact metaphor for the Javanese conception not only of the structure of the state but also of center-periphery relationships and of territorial sovereignty'. This model of 'graduated sovereignty' stands in contrast to its modern conceptions, in which power no longer exists on the other side of the border and where the power of the centre is 'theoretically uniform in weight' (Anderson 2007, 22, 29–30).

This understanding of power is influenced by the Sanskrit concept of the mandala. Academic discussion of the term mandala is generally considered to have begun with Wolters (1968), who described a fourteenth century Javanese poem in which the island was depicted at the centre of the Majapahit empire surrounded by Thai, Khmer and Cham vassal states. As he noted, however, the concept had a much longer history in Indic Southeast Asia, stretching back to ninth century Angkor. The mandala is also invoked through Tambiah's (1977, 1985) concept of the 'galactic polity', which he used to explain precolonial sovereignty in mainland Southeast Asia. This model of sovereignty incorporated both a secular monarch and a religious authority, wherein the religious authority bestowed its blessing on the monarch on the condition that he ruled in accordance with Buddhist teachings (Schobrer 1995). Many others have built on this understanding, for example, Stuart-Fox (1997), who used the model of the galactic polity to describe how pre-colonial Lao *muang*, or petty chiefdoms, functioned by garnering support through tribute and taxes from surrounding villages in exchange for military protection.

Another influential reading comes to us through Winichakul's (1994) description of the situated nature of sovereignty in the territory that is now Thailand. Prior to the late 1880s, the Siamese Court saw its kingdom as an agglomeration of towns separated by vacant territory, in effect an archipelago surrounded by a vast sea. Neighbouring kingdoms were separated by corridors of forest and mountains which lay beyond the boundaries of authority of either kingdom and thus constituted a border without boundary lines and without a frontier. Since no boundary line was recognised, the position of a guardhouse and the distance a guard could patrol from it defined the extent of Bangkok's reach. As such, the boundaries of sovereignty were not coterminous with a border, as the former was geographically well inside the latter, and the latter was beyond the limit of sovereign authority and without a boundary (Winichakul 1994).

Importantly, also, the sovereignty of this pre-modern polity was neither singular nor exclusive; it could be distributed among different rulers, as overlords shared sovereignty with tributary states in the buffer zones. Thus, in addition to spaces where no authority was exercised, there were spaces where power fields intersected, constituting a 'sovereignty of hierarchical layers' (Winichakul 1994, 88). This was a conception of boundaries and borders that stood in contrast to colonial understandings of territoriality and sovereignty in neighbouring Malaya, where the British insisted that a border marked the edge of state power. Maps became an essential tool in this process of demarcating boundaries and a device for new administrative mechanisms and for military purposes, in the process creating Siam as 'a new entity whose geo-body had never existed before' (Winichakul 1994, 130).

Sovereignty was much less clear-cut in some other European colonies in the region, most notably the Dutch East Indies. Van der Kroef (1958, 366) argued that from the 1870s the Dutch administration not only believed that it was sovereign but also 'coerced the Indonesian principalities to recognize this sovereignty' such that it not only managed external affairs but also had authority to intervene in the domestic affairs of those principalities. However, there have been challenges to this position. Working from the texts of official memoranda, ordinances, and legal sources, Resink (1968, 335) describes Dutch control of the archipelago as a 'dust cloud of sovereignties'. This assessment has also been questioned but, as Locher-Scholten (2004, 34) asserts, there is value in Resink's approach which 'sharpened our awareness of the varicoloured exercise of power within the archipelago'.

Acknowledgment of colonial-era graduated forms of sovereignty dimmed after Indonesia declared its independence in 1945; in practice, however, the capacity of successive governments to extend the reach of the state through the vast territories of the archipelago remains limited, in many ways reproducing the islands of authority that Tambiah (1985) described. Until today, the state's presence remains patchy in Indonesia's vast and varied borderlands. However, not all irregular border-crossings occur in spaces of state incapacity; many in fact occur in spaces of deliberate state absence (Ford and Lyons 2013) – as is nowhere more evident than at the Tawau–Nunukan border crossing in Borneo, where commercial ferry services routinely stop within sight of the Tawau port to allow undocumented returnees to board and again to allow them to alight before reaching the immigration checkpoint on the Indonesian side of the border (Field observations, May 2010).

2.2 As Borders Harden

In the second half of the twentieth century, the international community and individual countries began developing systems that accorded different groups of migrants, from permanent residents, to business and student visa-holders, to refugees and irregular migrants, with 'varying civil and social rights' (Morris-Suzuki 2006, 15). As Castles (2011, 318) notes, these systems of categorisation underpinned a 'new transnational class structure' in which the 'right' passports and qualifications open the door to 'mobility rights which come close to global citizenship' while the wrong ones leave individuals with little choice but to accept much lesser conditions or to 'move irregularly, running enormous risks'.

The intersection between different border-crossing identities allows states to cherry-pick labels in order to maximise their ability to deal with migrants in ways they see as politically beneficial. Around the world, governments have defined asylum seekers as economic migrants as a way of denying the moral validity of their claims for asylum. The Israeli government describes African asylum-seekers as economic migrants, arguing that protections in refugee law do not apply to them (Voss 2018). The government of the United Kingdom has also used assertions that asylum seekers are economic migrants both to justify the denial of their claims and to argue that their legal representatives are helping them to abuse the law (Zimmermann 2011). The government in Hungary, too, has claimed that asylum seekers are 'illegal economic migrants' as a way of justifying tighter border controls, although evidence shows that most people seeking asylum genuinely fear persecution (Tetenyi, Barczikay and Szent-Ivanyi 2018). As these examples attest, it is not only Southeast Asian countries that have blurred this distinction to control refugee flows – but it is certainly a feature of border management in the region.

The prevailing global approach to migration deeply privileges countries' desire to maintain sovereignty through control of their borders. As McKeown (2012, 38) observes:

> Even as immigration restrictions based on race are disappearing, discrimination based on place of birth, wealth, education and family is not only tolerated but encouraged. A globalizing class that is free to cross borders is emerging hand in hand with an impoverished and uneducated class whose movement is possible only under conditions of severe restrictions, surveillance or illegality.

But, even after the advent of modern borders, Southeast Asians continued to traverse them largely unhindered. For example, large numbers of Laotians cross the border to work on nearby Thai farms (Rungmanee 2016). These border-crossers are well-received because of a shared cultural history and, although they are undocumented, neither the workers nor the farmers who employ them perceive them as engaging in illegal activities. Nevertheless, first anti-trafficking programmes and then the COVID-19 pandemic worked to restrict this community's ability to engage in cross-border mobility.

Like Thailand, Malaysia has a long land border (in Borneo), but also long sea borders (with Indonesia and its mainland Southeast Asian neighbours). There is an assumption that crossing a sea border is more arduous and time-consuming than crossing a land border, but this is not necessarily so. Indeed, from parts of Indonesia, Malaysia and Singapore are as little as half an hour away by boat (Ford and Lyons 2009).[2] This maritime border, a division based on colonial spheres of trade and influence rather than pre-existing cultural or political boundaries, was originally established as a 'line of demarcation' under the Anglo-Dutch Treaty of 1824. Under this treaty, the Dutch agreed that the British would have the right to influence the Malay Peninsula, the island of Singapore at its tip and Dutch Sumatra, including the Riau Islands. Over time, this 'line of demarcation' evolved into a border between their respective colonial territories and, much later, between current-day Singapore, Malaysia and Indonesia (Ford and Lyons 2009).

Until the 1960s, individuals crossed these straits regularly and with little regard for the markers of territorial sovereignty or jurisdiction, following well-travelled trade routes established during pre-colonial times and strengthened by

[2] This discussion draws on Ford and Lyons (2012a).

the presence of Chinese migrants who began moving into the region in the 1800s (Tagliacozzo 2007). After independence, residents of Indonesia's Riau Islands continued to trade with both Malaysia and Singapore. Some of this trade was sanctioned, but much of it was not. When Lenore Lyons and I were conducting fieldwork on the island of Karimun, I interviewed a Malay teacher who regaled me with stories of how he became rich from the illegal export of copra in the 1950s. Many other older people I spoke to had also engaged in some kind of illegal cross-border trade. These included Hamzah, a 62-year-old Bugis fisher living in northern Bintan, who sold dried coconut and fish in Singapore and bought rice, sugar and clothes in return. According to Sugiyanto, a Javanese migrant I spoke to in Tanjung Pinang, travelling to Singapore in the late 1950s to sell a few kilograms of chillies or rubber was 'just like going to the market ... there were no obstacles, and no-one bothered us'.

In fact, it was only in 1963, with the tensions that accompanied what became known as the period of *Konfrontasi* between Indonesia and Malaya, that practices of sovereignty became more closely linked with boundary maintenance along this border (Ford and Lyons 2009). The Riau Islands were not a war zone, but *Konfrontasi* certainly had the effect of shutting the border down (Ng 1976). As Hamzah recall,

> During *Konfrontasi* it became really hard to get to and from the islands, so it was very difficult to keep our relationships with Singapore going. As a result, we really suffered economically. It was very difficult to get even basic necessities. Sometimes we'd have the money to buy food, and there'd simply be none that we could buy.

For Riau Islanders, then, it was *Konfrontasi*, rather than the establishment of Indonesia as an independent nation-state, that was pivotal in marking the new 'national' border between Indonesia, and what was then part of Malaya (Ford and Lyons 2006).

This new border not only restricted movement across the Straits; it also made people on either side of the border more aware of their status as citizens. However, sovereignty and jurisdiction remained works in progress in the border zone. As relations between Indonesia and the newly independent nations of Malaysia and Singapore began to normalise, people resumed movement across the Straits. Older residents told us that they still did not need a passport to enter Singapore, although they were required to have their photograph taken and were given a stamp at the immigration post that allowed them to stay in Singapore for forty-eight hours. It was not until well into the 1970s that the process of border-crossing routinely involved passport and customs controls. And, even then, the border remained incredibly porous. Kasiyem, a resident of Tanjung Balai, had spent twenty years in Malaysia working on an oil palm plantation as an undocumented worker. Throughout that period, she and her husband would travel back and forth from the Riau Islands illegally by boat, and without a passport. Dasril, who also travelled illegally for work in the 1980s, reported that fellow islanders would travel illegally to Malaysia up to three times a day to smuggle cigarettes and other goods across the border into Indonesia.

This is not to suggest that the borders were not policed at all during this period, as evidenced by the case of Yusuf, a man who had been recently banned from Singapore for holding two passports in a different name when I interviewed him in 2006. More than a decade earlier, Yusuf had worked illegally for two years in Singapore's construction industry. Upon his return from a holiday in the Riau Islands, he was arrested and imprisoned for entering Singapore without proper papers. At another time, he had been stopped by customs with a boatload of contraband cigarettes in Singaporean waters. On that occasion, he and some members of his crew avoided capture by throwing the cigarettes overboard and swimming for over eight hours to get to Batam – an ordeal that two crew members did not survive.

In more recent decades, the region's borders remained permeable, but their symbolic power grew – and, with it, their increased securitisation. In addition to concerns about Islamist terrorism in the 2000s and COVID-19 in the 2020s, pressure on Southeast Asian states to address human trafficking fed into an increased concern with policing their borders (Ford, Lyons and van Schendel 2012). Again, the Indonesia–Singapore borderlands case is instructive. In the early–mid 2000s, there were real fears that Islamist terrorists would target Singapore's harbour and oil refineries with 'floating bombs', or that the Singaporean-owned resort zone on the Indonesian island of Bintan would become another Bali (Ford and Lyons 2009) – a reference to the bombings of two Kuta tourist haunts in October 2002, in which 202 people died and another 209 were injured (West 2008). In those years, I remember being on ferries travelling from Tanjung Pinang and Batam that were stopped and inspected by armed coastguards before berthing in Singapore. Once travel resumed after the first flush of the COVID-19 pandemic, there was a period where it was possible to transit by air through the city-state without quarantining, but not by sea. During this time, Singapore was effectively closed to Indonesians living in the Riau islands.

The hardening of these borders has affected citizens of different countries very differently. For example, Singaporeans and Malaysians pass through Indonesian checkpoints without being questioned, but every Indonesian who seeks to enter Singapore or Malaysia risks being turned back (Ford and Lyons 2009). This risk is, however, parsed by other factors, including gender and class.

Over the decades, I have had many opportunities to observe the behaviour of immigration officials at Singapore's Tanah Merah port, where ferries from Tanjung Pinang berth. The papers of all Indonesians passing through this and other seaports were always examined more closely than of Indonesians arriving by air. But it was patently obvious that wealthy, well-presented people, both men and women, passed much more easily through the Tanah Merah immigration checkpoint than working-class Indonesians.

Working-class women suspected of entering Singapore to work in the sex industry or in domestic service were generally more likely to be held up at immigration checkpoints at Tanah Merah or Harbour Front (where the ferries from Batam and Karimun berth) than working-class men. The exception was during the terrorism years, when the ferry ports in Karimun, Batam and Bintan were plastered with wanted posters featuring pictures of prominent and lesser-known terrorists. One the posters I photographed in Karimun featured Azahari, the Afghanistan-trained Malaysian national accused of masterminding a series of bombings across Indonesia. The poster featured an image and a detailed description noting, amongst other things, his thick glasses and thin moustache, but also the fact that he spoke with a Malay accent and always carried a small black bag. Another featured Azahari's co-conspirator, Noordin Top, also a Malaysian, described as being of stocky build and having 'bright yellow' skin, wavy hair and acne-marked skin. In this period, men seeking to enter Singapore by sea from Indonesia were far more likely to be scrutinised than women.

3 Drivers of Cross-border Mobility

Cross-border mobility is born of a complex set of factors that varies by country but also by class and individual circumstance. Most migrants exert some level of agency in deciding whether to stay or to try to leave. However, opportunities to live and work abroad differ by country of origin, even for members of the educated middle class. Architects and engineers from Australia, Germany and the United States of America – or Singapore, for that matter – face far lower barriers to cross-border mobility than equally skilled members of those professions from Laos, Vietnam or Cambodia. But the variation in the kinds of mobility available to the world's highly educated is smaller than the variation in experience between the richest and poorest members of society in countries of the Global South. This is not to say that only the wealthy and educated are mobile, but rather to underscore the structural and cultural constraints that dictate how, and in what circumstances, people at different levels of society can cross borders.

Regardless of socio-economic status, cross-border mobility may be driven by a multitude of different factors including a desire to broaden one's horizons, to improve one's economic situation or to escape stigma or political oppression. Even wealthy or highly educated people may be compelled to leave. Artists and intellectuals can become the targets of state-sanctioned violence in repressive societies, and even professionals may feel that they have no choice but to leave if inflation spirals to levels where they cannot feed their family, or it feels impossible to keep them safe. At the other end of the spectrum, the poorest of the poor may not have the wherewithal to depart. Equally, they may not have the choice to stay if they are forced across a border by a genocidal state or become caught up in a trafficking ring. However, many border-crossers of the Global South are neither wealthy nor very poor.

As Angenendt and Koch (2017) observe, then, border controls alone do not determine migratory movements. Border-crossing is, rather, underpinned by a much broader tapestry of factors including everything from global trade regimes and uneven development to political turmoil, social conservatism, and environmental disasters. In the decades since Southeast Asia's national borders began to be policed, dominant forms of non-proximate cross-border mobility have been sparked by the region's high levels of political instability and internal conflict, but also the vast inequalities in and between countries. These inequalities fuel not only the region's structural dependence on temporary labour migration, but also other patterns of mobility, including the pathways that refugees take. But before addressing the question of how governments manage these different groups of border-crossers, it is important to first consider the fundamental drivers of various forms of cross-border mobility.

3.1 Political Drivers

When we think of political drivers of cross-border mobility in Southeast Asia, the case that first springs to mind is Myanmar, which has for decades been the source of the vast majority of the region's refugees (Henry 2018). However, there are many political drivers of regional cross-border mobility besides the outright persecution experienced by democracy activists and ethnic minorities in that country. Instability in several Southeast Asian countries has generated significant refugee flows. Millions of people fled from the former French colonies of Indochina after the Communists seized power. A mass exodus from Vietnam began in 1975, just before the fall of Saigon. By 1980, over a quarter of a million people had fled the regime (Osborne 1980).[3] In neighbouring Cambodia,

[3] A significant proportion were Hmong, a highland minority that had supported the United States in covert operations conducted between 1961 and 1973 (Vang 2016).

hundreds of thousands of people were internally displaced and over 320,000 fled the country from 1975 to 79, the brutal period of rule by the Khmer Rouge (Osborne 1980). After Vietnam invaded in early 1979, tens of thousands more crossed the border into Thailand, only to be pushed back by Thai soldiers into the minefields on the Cambodian side of the border (Hedman 2008). As fighting between the Vietnamese and Khmer Rouge intensified, more people tried to enter Thailand (Davies 2008).

Refugee flows from Myanmar also began in the 1970s, with small numbers of mostly Karen villagers fleeing conflict zones (Moretti 2015).[4] More left in 1984, and again in the early 1990s, as the Burmese military intensified its response to separatist groups (Decobert 2016). While the majority of refugees were Karen, significant numbers of Karenni, Mon and Shan also fled (Moretti 2015). A different kind of refugee then emerged in the late 1980s, when some 10,000 students and activists involved in the failed 1988 democracy uprising fled to the Thai border regions (South 2008) – alongside the Christian minority population of Chin State, who had been politically disenfranchised and persecuted by the junta (Murugasu 2017). Continued clashes between the state and ethnic minorities led to an increase in refugee flows from some parts of Myanmar during the 1990s and 2000s, and into the 2010s. For example, intense fighting between the military and the Arakan Army in 2019 had devastating consequences for civilians, prompting further departures among the Chin (UNHRC 2019).

Overall, many fewer refugees left Myanmar once it began its transition from overt military rule in 2011. However, the opposite has been the case for the Muslim Rohingya, whom successive Myanmar governments have long claimed are illegal immigrants. The exodus began in 1978, when a military operation resulted in some 200,000 members of that community fleeing to Bangladesh. Four years later, the Rohingya were made formally stateless by the Burma Citizenship Act of 1982, which excluded them from the list of recognised national ethnic groups. Since then, they have been subjected to severe restrictions of movement and denied the right to marry, and suffered from confiscation of land, forced labour and inadequate health and education services (Lewa 2008). These conditions have resulted in repeated waves of departures (Zarni and Cowley 2014). In 2012, more than 140,000 people were displaced when the government increased its security force presence, segregated communities, and further limited their already restricted movement (UNHRC 2018). The crisis intensified in May 2015, when thousands of Rohingya were abandoned by people smugglers at sea, only to be pushed back by Indonesia, Malaysia and

[4] For details of Myanmar's political history, the initial transition and subsequent transfer of power to the National League for Democracy, see David and Holliday (2018)

Thailand (Wake 2016; Wake and Cheung 2016). However, the largest displacements in a decade were yet to occur.

In August 2017, Myanmar's armed forces responded to an armed attack on a military base by launching what it described as 'clearance operations', which forced as many as 730,000 more refugees to cross the border to camps in Bangladesh (UNHRC 2018). These repeated acts of persecution decimated the Rohingya community, which shrank from 1 to 1.5 million to just 600,000 between 2014 and 2019 (ERT 2014; UNHRC 2018).[5] Just when numbers had settled, the military ousted the civilian government and again seized power, prompting a further wave of Rohingya and other refugees from Myanmar.

Conflict in Muslim-dominated areas in the south of the Philippines and Thailand and the separatist region of Aceh in Indonesia also produced refugee flows (Amer and Zou 2011; Yusuf 2007; Missbach 2012). In addition, tens of thousands of East Timorese fled after Indonesia annexed the territory in 1975, including the more than 11,000 who sought sanctuary in Australia (Wise 2006). A further 240,000 sought temporary sanctuary in West Timor in response to large-scale outbreaks of violence after the independence ballot of 1999 (McDowell and Eastmond 2002). While seldom formally considered to be refugees, up to 4 per cent of Indonesia's ethnic Chinese sought work or study opportunities in other countries as a way of leaving Indonesia after they became targets of mass riots across the country in the final weeks of the Suharto regime in 1998 (Purdey 2005; Winarnita et al. 2020).

Other political drivers of cross-border mobility push persecuted individuals to either formally seek asylum or leave using personal and family resources. One such form is other manifestations of religious persecution, whether it be government sanctions against atheism in Indonesia and Malaysia, restrictions on the establishment of churches in Indonesia or the equation of Muslim identity with being Malay in Malaysia (Fealy 2019; Siddique 1981). Another is campaigns against male homosexuality, which was criminalised in Malaysia and Singapore in colonial times. While Singapore has recently decriminalised homosexual acts, they remain illegal in Malaysia. Men who have sex with men have also become a target for legal and vigilante oppression in Indonesia in recent years (Wijaya and Davies 2019). Dozens of individuals from Southeast Asia have sought asylum in countries in the Global North on the basis of their

[5] An independent fact-finding mission concluded that the treatment of the Rohingya by the military amounted to genocide, and that senior officers should be investigated and prosecuted on this basis (UNHRC 2018). The International Criminal Court also launched an investigation into crimes against humanity allegedly committed by Myanmar's military and authorities against the Rohingya and there is a case in the International Court of Justice regarding Myanmar's alleged genocide (Renshaw 2019).

sexual orientation (Offord 2013). These claims are seldom successful, though Canada and the United Kingdom have granted asylum to some gay Malaysians and Indonesians (Sheldrick 2016; Pidd 2019; Varagur 2019).

3.2 Environmental Drivers

Environmental factors are also increasingly at play in a region threatened by rising sea levels and other climate-related disasters, including drought, floods and life-threatening storms. From the tsunami that decimated Aceh to Myanmar's Cyclone Nargis – but also droughts in the Mekong Delta and Eastern Indonesia and annual flooding in the Philippines and elsewhere – natural disasters have killed or displaced millions of people and caused serious economic damage across Southeast Asia. Vietnam and Indonesia are among the top ten countries globally in terms of the number of people at risk of displacement as a consequence of rises in sea levels, and river deltas in Myanmar, Thailand and Cambodia are also under threat (Wennerstein and Robbins 2017). And, while not facing as immediate danger as the Pacific or Bangladesh, the region is deeply exposed to the impact of climate change, both as a consequence of its geography and because of its relatively high levels of poverty and the state of its physical and social infrastructure.[6]

Globally, climate migration looms large in the international imagination, with estimates of up to 250 million people at risk of displacement by 2050 (Francis and Maguire 2013). Debates around climate refugees reflect the same tension between the international system's emphasis on sovereignty and its emphasis on rights, with the United Nations High Commissioner for Refugees (UNHCR) acknowledging the risks of displacement associated with climate change and natural disasters but rejecting the term 'climate refugee' (UNHCR 2020a).[7] As Elmhirst et al. (2017, 2) note, influential studies of climate change have challenged 'simplistic and inaccurate assessments of the links between environmental hazards and accelerated rates of cross-border and transnational migration'. It is indeed important not to fall prey to alarmist estimates of climate-induced migration, which can fuel states' security agendas and thus reduce mobility options for those affected (McAdam 2012). At the same time, however, the deep tensions between climate-induced threats to state and human security are acutely evident in Southeast Asia (Gerstl and Helmke 2012).

[6] For a discussion of the multi-causality of forced migration and the challenges of establishing the case for climate refugees, see Zetter (2010).

[7] For an academic analysis of debates around terms like climate refugees, see McAdam (2012).

To date, most environmental displacement has occurred within national borders (McAdam 2012; Obokata et al. 2014). However, some already involves border-crossing – as evidenced by increases in the rate of labour migration from Cambodia to Thailand in years following drought, poor rainfall or crop loss (Bylander 2016) – and such behaviours are likely to increase. Importantly, also natural disasters and climate change hit hardest in poorer countries, which have less institutional capacity to withstand their impact (Millock 2015). It is these countries that are most likely to become sources of international climate refugees.

3.3 Economic Drivers

While asylum seekers and refugees are perhaps the most visible group of border-crossers, the 'overwhelming majority' of the world's migrants leave their home countries 'voluntarily in search of economic opportunities' (World Bank 2017, 16). It is clear that one factor is the paucity of employment opportunities as a consequence of uneven development, high rates of unemployment and education systems that do not adequately prepare young people for employment. Many countries in Southeast Asia experienced high levels of rural to urban migration from the 1970s to the 2010s, as they turned to labour-intensive export-oriented manufacturing as a source of employment and economic growth. However, internal migration is not always enough in contexts where the demand for jobs outstrips their availability. And, despite the potential hardships associated with working overseas, the opportunity to do so is an attractive option for individuals who can earn much higher wages than at home for much the same work – whether it be in households, on rubber or palm oil plantations, or in the construction, manufacturing or services sectors (Ford 2019).

Another factor that encourages economic migration is the presence of economic disparities between countries. With a GDP of USD 1.042 trillion in 2018, Indonesia's economy is more than twice the size of Thailand's, the region's second-largest economy (World Bank 2020a), although Thailand's GDP per capita is close to double Indonesia's. Singapore meanwhile has one of the highest GDP per capita in the world.[8] At the other end of the spectrum is Timor-Leste, with a GDP per capita of just USD 1,237 (Table 1).

[8] As of 2018, Singapore had the twelfth highest GDP per capita in the world. The only relatively large countries with a higher GDP per capita are Switzerland, Norway, Iceland and Qatar. The remainder are European principalities and tax havens (World Bank 2020b).

Table 1 Labour force participation and GDP per capita, 2018

	Labour force participation				
	Population (million)	**Labour force (million)**	**Male (%)**	**Female (%)**	**GDP per capita (USD)**
Singapore	5.6	3.5	78.4	62.1	66,189
Brunei	0.4	0.2	71.4	57.9	31,628
Malaysia	31.5	15.4	77.0	50.6	11,373
Thailand	69.4	38.9	76.3	59.4	7,295
Indonesia	267.7	132.7	82.0	53.0	3,894
Philippines	106.7	43.9	73.3	46.0	3,252
Vietnam	95.5	56.9	82.5	72.8	2,567
Laos	7.1	3.7	80.2	76.7	2,542
Cambodia	16.2	9.2	88.7	76.3	1,512
Myanmar	53.7	24.5	77.6	47.7	1,418
Timor-Leste	1.3	0.5	72.8	61.9	1,237

Note: Labour force participation rates are modelled estimates by the International Labour Organization (ILO)

Source: World Bank (2020a).

The job opportunities and wage differentials associated with these disparities make economic migration attractive to individuals and the families, but also to governments as a means of reducing unemployment rates, and thus reducing pressure on their labour markets. In addition, overseas contract work can prop up an economy through remittances. The Philippines is among the top ten remittance-receiving countries globally, generating remittances worth USD 33.8 billion, or 9.8 per cent GDP, in 2018 (IOM 2019, 36). In Vietnam, remittances worth USD 15.9 billion accounted for 6.5 per cent of its GDP in the same year (IOM 2019, World Bank 2020a). While remittances account for a smaller percentage of GDP for other countries in the region, including Indonesia, they are nevertheless highly significant in migrant-sending communities (Ford 2019). Sometimes these remittances make little difference to the long-term well-being of temporary migrants and their families. Often, however, they provide a resource base for class mobility that would not otherwise be available, including the means to build comfortable houses, begin businesses and equip the next generation to achieve a better standard of living without having to migrate for work.

4 Managing Cross-border Flows

States' management of border-crossers is highly political, even when ostensibly driven by economic considerations. More than technocratic challenges like border policing or labour market demand, domestic politics and even international relations drive the region's bordering regimes. At its heart is the distinction between refugees and migrants, which:

> echoes a political discourse that in many countries is more specifically focused on controlling *irregular* migration – cross-border movement of people not authorised, and at times criminalised, by receiving states. The dominant narrative on irregular migration often posits a binary classification that is expressed in a variety of paired terms, contrasting victims with criminals, or forced with voluntary or economic migration. Migrants are thus divided into those deserving particular protections and assistance, and others who are undeserving or even threatening, hence justifying defensive measures by states. (Meyer and Boll 2018, 4–5)

This point is underscored by the distinction made internationally and by governments between smuggled and trafficked border-crossers. Under international law, both human trafficking and people smuggling are identified as forms of criminal activity. They are, however, distinguished by the locus of agency, defined as the presence or absence of consent (Ford, Lyons and van Schendel 2012). The Trafficking Protocol defines trafficking in persons as 'the recruitment, transportation, transfer, harbouring or receipt of persons, by means of the threat or use of force or other forms of coercion, of abduction, of fraud, of deception, of the abuse of power or of a position of vulnerability or of the giving or receiving of payments or benefits to achieve the consent of a person having control over another person, for the purpose of exploitation' (UNODC 2000). The concept of consent is, however, ill-defined and slippery, making it deeply vulnerable to politicisation (Meyer and Boll 2018, 6–7).

The Trafficking Protocol may have shifted the focus from victims to traffickers, but punishment of traffickers is mandatory while victim protection and assistance are left to the discretion of the relevant state.[9] And, since repatriation is the mandated endpoint of a 'rescue' operation, the default remedy for those identified as victims of trafficking – whether they be failed asylum seekers, labour migrants, or actual trafficked persons – is repatriation, which may place individuals in an even more vulnerable position, facing stigma, outstanding debt

[9] Other parts of the United Nations system, including the Office of the High Commissioner for Human Rights, have attempted to restore focus on the rights of trafficked persons (OHCHR 2002).

or even mortal threat. And, perhaps most importantly, the anti-trafficking approach diverts governments' focus from the broader task of reforming the structures that encourage the exploitation of border-crossers in the first place.

In theory, a clear line can be drawn between refugees, economic migrants seeking a better life and victims of trafficking. But, in practice, the distinction between those who *need* and those who *want* admission to another country is deeply problematic. People fleeing the threat of political persecution who fail to secure refugee status frequently end up working illegally in a second or third country. Even those who are recognised as refugees may engage in unauthorised employment, and so are vulnerable to the same conditions of precarity, exploitation and abuse as irregular migrant workers. Moreover, as economic migrants and refugees increasingly travel the same routes and use the services of the same smugglers, there is often also little to distinguish their experiences *en route* to their first or final destination (Crisp 2008).

4.1 Asylum Seekers and Refugees

Policies towards refugees in Southeast Asia's host countries have their genesis in the experience of dealing with the millions of people who fled Indochina from the mid-1970s. Over the following two decades, more than three million people from Vietnam, Cambodia and Laos fled north to Hong Kong and Mainland China or to other parts of Southeast Asia (McConnahie 2014).[10] Although Indonesia and the Philippines were affected, Thailand, and to a lesser extent, Malaysia, bore the brunt of the crisis. Initially, these Indochinese refugees were allowed temporary first asylum in Southeast Asia on the understanding that they would be guaranteed resettlement in a third country (Betts 2011). Responding to a tightening of Western countries' stance on refugee status, a new agreement was put in place in 1989, under which *prima facie* refugee status was no longer granted, and instead asylum seekers were to be screened by member states of the Association of Southeast Asian Nations (ASEAN). This change in policy resulted in the large-scale repatriations of so-called non-genuine refugees (Davies 2008).

As a consequence of their relative prosperity and geographical proximity to areas that have experienced political upheaval and/or economic turmoil in recent decades, Thailand and Malaysia – neither of which has ratified the Refugee Convention – bear the burden of large-scale displacement from other

[10] Even earlier, many ethnic Chinese had been pushed to leave Vietnam following the introduction of anti-Chinese policies in the late 1960s (Lam 2000). Ultimately, a quarter of a million people were resettled in China, while many more fled to neighbouring countries within Southeast Asia.

countries in Southeast Asia.[11] As of 2018, there were over 2.3 million people of concern to the UNHCR in Southeast Asia. Myanmar and the Philippines were host to significant populations of internally displaced persons, and Myanmar, Cambodia, Malaysia and tiny Brunei to substantial numbers of stateless persons. Asylum seekers and refugees, meanwhile, were concentrated in Malaysia and Thailand, with just over 14,000 more in Indonesia (Table 2).

Having accommodated millions of Indochinese refugees in the 1970s, 1980s and 1990s, Thailand became the primary destination for large numbers of refugees of different ethnic minority backgrounds from Myanmar. The refugee flows from Myanmar to Thailand began around the same time as the Indochinese crisis, with small numbers of mostly Karen villagers fleeing conflict zones and abuse by the army (Moretti 2015). More refugees began to cross the border in 1984, and again in the early 1990s as the Burmese military intensified its response to separatist groups (Decobert 2016). Although many live in the community, refugees from Myanmar have been officially confined to Thailand's border camps (Okudaira and Nasu 2013).[12]

As Banki and Lang (2008, 59) have noted, these camps 'represent the largest protracted refugee situation in East Asia'. By the mid-1990s, the last of the camps established for refugees from Indochina had closed. But, in the meantime, nine camps had been established to house refugees from Myanmar. As of late 2007, these camps housed 153,000 registered refugees from various ethnic groups, most of whom were Karen (Banki and Lang 2008). By the end of 2010, the camp population had declined to 95,330, due to resettlement in third countries (Chantavanich 2011). While more than 100,000 refugees were eventually resettled, the camp population in Thailand remained stable because of continued periodic conflict across the border in Myanmar. As of May 2019, there were approximately 121,000 refugees in the camps (UNHRC 2019).

[11] As of 2022, only Cambodia, the Philippines and Timor-Leste – none of which are the countries to which refugees flee – were signatories to the Refugee Convention. The Australian government tried to negotiate deals with Cambodia, Indonesia, Malaysia and Timor-Leste to take refugees as an alternative to its so-called Pacific Solution. With the exception of Cambodia, these agreements failed to come to fruition – and, in that case, only a handful of refugees accepted settlement there, all but one of whom quickly moved on.

[12] The strategy of encampment is one of three main elements in Thailand's approach to refugees (Chantavanich 2011). The second is to collaborate with international donors, who help defray the costs associated with the refugee presence. The third is to encourage repatriation. A voluntary repatriation programme established unilaterally in 2005 but failed because Myanmar was not yet safe. Over a decade later, Myanmar and Thailand agreed to facilitate voluntary repatriation, but by the end of 2018 only two small groups of refugees had returned home through the official programme (Harkins 2019).

Table 2 People of concern to the UNHCR in Southeast Asia, 2018

Country	IDPs	Returnees	Stateless Persons	Asylum Seekers	Refugees	Others	All People of Concern
Cambodia	0	0	57,444	0	0	0	57,444
Laos	0	0	0	0	0	0	0
Myanmar	370,305	474	495,939	0	0	0	866,718
Philippines	77,650	445,655	1,068	248	642	68	525,331
Timor-Leste	0	0	0	0	0	2	2
Vietnam	0	0	0	34,110	0	0	34,110
Brunei	0	0	20,863	0	0	0	20,863
Indonesia	0	0	0	3,223	10,793	0	14,016
Malaysia	0	0	9,631	41,809	121,302	80,000	252,742
Thailand	0	0	478,843	944	102,245	98	582,130
Regional	447,955	446,129	1,063,788	80,334	234,982	80,168	2,353,356

Source: Data from UNHCR Statistics (2020).

Although accommodating a much lower number of refugees in 2020 than Thailand did at its peak, relative to population size, Malaysia has dealt with a much higher number of refugees in the last two decades – and from 2014 more in absolute terms (UNHCR Statistics 2020). Malaysia's refugee population comes from a more diverse range of ethnic and national backgrounds than those found in Thailand. However, Malaysia has been particularly open to Muslims from other countries in the region. Well before the Indochinese crisis, Malaysia accepted Muslim refugees from the southern Philippines (Amer and Zou 2011). Then, in the early 1970s, around 100,000 refugees from Mindanao were granted permission to stay in the Eastern Malaysian state of Sabah (Kassim 2009). This policy had the blessing of the Federal Government, with the Foreign Affairs Minister noting that their presence would not cause any 'adverse consequences' because they were Muslims of the same ethnic background as the Peninsular Malays (Murugasu 2017). Refugees from the Southern Philippines have continued to flee to Malaysia, including some 50,000 civilians who arrived in 2000 after fighting flared up between the Philippine government and the Moro Islamic Liberation Front (Amer and Zou 2011).

Other Muslims who have made their way to Malaysia include Cham fleeing Vietnam in the 1970s and 1980s; Southern Thais, who sought asylum in Malaysia's northern states (Yusuf 2007; Hoffstaedter 2017); and the Acehnese from Indonesia, who came in increasing numbers when the conflict in their home province became more violent from the late 1970s onwards (Missbach 2012). By the early 1990s, there were at least 2,000 Acehnese in the country, including both fighters from the Free Aceh Movement and civilians escaping the deteriorating security situation and thousands more Acehnese fled to Malaysia when the conflict flared again in 1999.[13] However, the largest group of Muslim refugees has been the Rohingya, who accounted for over half of the nearly 180,000 individuals registered with the UNHCR as of March 2020 (UNHCR 2020b). There is, moreover, evidence of Rohingya arriving in Malaysia as early as 1982 (FIDH and SUARAM 2008).[14]

It is also common for asylum seekers from the Middle East and elsewhere to enter Malaysia and then travel to Indonesia before attempting to reach Australia

[13] See Missbach (2012) for detailed accounts of the experiences of several Acehnese refugees in Malaysia.

[14] Another large group from the Myanmar are the Christian Chin, who accounted for around one-eighth of Malaysia's registered refugee population in March 2020 (UNHCR 2020b). The UNHCR also recognised the Chin as a vulnerable group and, in contrast to the Rohingya, their waiting times for permanent resettlement have been relatively short (Hoffstaedter 2014). Over the course of the 2000s, almost 40,000 Chins were resettled in the United States, Canada, Australia and Scandinavia (Murugasu 2017).

by boat.[15] Like Malaysia and Thailand, Indonesia has not ratified the Refugee Convention. Two-thirds of asylum seekers there live in immigration detention centres, with the remainder living in the community in straightened circumstances (Prabandari and Adiputera 2019). Conditions in government facilities range 'from acceptable to appalling' (Taylor 2009, 4). Asylum seekers are prohibited from engaging in income-generating activities and are unable to access education or healthcare. In addition, they are routinely detained without legal advice (Tan 2016). A significant problem facing detainees is lengthy delays in processing by the UNHCR, waiting up to thirty-six months for a refugee status determination, and then having little prospect of third country settlement (Taylor 2009).[16]

While none of Southeast Asia's destination countries for asylum seekers have ratified the Refugee Convention, Southeast Asia nevertheless offers 'a myriad of forms of refuge', reflecting 'informal, tacit and often localized understandings in borderlands and frontier towns, in provincial and national urban centres' that allow for 'varying degrees of everyday forms of incorporation into local political economies, social networks and even, in places, electoral machines' (Hedman 2008, 358–9). At the same time, these cross-border flows of asylum seekers and refugees have had a negative impact on bilateral relationships. Before 2011, the presence of refugees from Myanmar in Thailand caused tension in the relationship between the two countries, and the Thai government periodically used them as a bargaining chip in negotiations (Brees 2010). Similarly, although the relationship between Malaysia and Indonesia is normally governed by the principle of non-interference, the relationship was strained for many years by what the Indonesian government saw as Malaysia's failure to hand over Acehnese separatists, or to prevent them from smuggling arms from Thailand into Aceh (Missbach 2012).

4.2 Temporary Labour Migrants

The second main group of border-crossers in the region are temporary labour migrants. All the poorer countries in the region have embraced low-skilled temporary labour migration as part of their development strategy, giving rise to what Rodriguez (2010) describes as the 'brokerage state', in which governments

[15] As of early 2020, there were 6,690 Pakistanis, 3,720 Yemenis, 3,310 Somalis, 3,300 Syrians, 2,660 Afghans, 1,820 Sri Lankans, 1,270 Iraqis and 790 Palestinians registered with the UNHCR in Malaysia (UNHCR 2020b). There were approximately 13,500 asylum seekers registered in Indonesia, including 7,668 Afghans, 1,421 Somalis, 441 Sri Lankans, 339 Pakistanis, and 2,001 people from various parts of the Middle East (UNHCR Indonesia 2020).

[16] The flow of refugees through Malaysia and Indonesia has also long been a source of political tension. For details see Ford, Lyons and Palmer (2010) and Missbach (2018). For further details of conditions for asylum seekers in Indonesia, see Hugo, Tan and Napitupulu (2014).

channel commodified labour into the global marketplace. The Philippines is the exemplar of this model, channelling many millions of workers abroad rather than finding ways to increase jobs at home (Rodriguez 2010). Indonesia followed suit, developing a complex system in which bilateral labour export agreements signed by governments are implemented primarily through the private sector from the early 1980s (Palmer 2016). From that time, temporary labour migration became a large-scale industry, with departures through official channels reaching their height in 2007, when 696,746 labour migrants left Indonesia (BNP2TKI 2014; World Bank 2007).

The countries of mainland Southeast Asia were slower to establish formal systems of labour export. Inspired by programmes in the Philippines and Indonesia, the Cambodian government began regulating and encouraging labour migration in 1995, setting up public companies for recruiting, training and sending migrant labours, as well as regulating private companies that perform these functions (Derks 2011). The Vietnamese government has managed different types of labour migration, first to Eastern Europe and since the 1990s migrants to the Middle East and Asia (IOM 2003). Laos developed a more modest scheme as part of its 2008 poverty reduction strategy (IMF 2008). Myanmar, meanwhile, has attempted to manage migrant labour for decades but has yet to develop a coherent labour export programme (ILO 2017).

In terms of absolute numbers, Southeast Asia's main countries of origin are the Philippines and Indonesia, followed by Vietnam, Cambodia, Laos and Myanmar. Many temporary labour migrants from these countries find their way to the Middle East, or to Northeast Asia. However, many more find work in Singapore, Malaysia and Thailand (Table 3).[17]

Among the region's destination countries, Malaysia was the first to actively manage inflows of labour migrants from the late 1960s (Kaur 2014). It has since offered employment for sizeable numbers of foreign workers in all key sectors of the economy, as well as in domestic service. This does not mean that workers can come from just anywhere, or work where they please. As of 2020, nationals of fifteen countries in South, Southeast and Central Asia between the ages of 18 and 45 could apply for a work permit in Malaysia. In most cases they could be recruited in any sector available under the scheme; however, Bangladeshi workers could only work on plantations and Indian workers could only be employed in a limited number of occupations outside the plantation sector. Women from the Philippines could not be employed outside domestic service, which is also available to nationals of Cambodia, India, Indonesia, Laos, Sri

[17] Malaysia and Thailand are also in the top fifteen Asian source countries for migration to OECD countries, with Thailand sending 61,500 migrants and Malaysia sending 23,400 migrants to work abroad (ADB, ILO and OECD 2016).

Table 3 Regular labour migrants by region of origin, 2019

	Malaysia[a]	**Thailand**	**Singapore**[b]
Population	31.2 million	69.6 million	5.7 million
Labour force	15.4 million	38.2 million	3.7 million
Total regular labour migrants	1,747,315	2,788,316	1,233,800
Total ASEAN labour migrants	882,949	2,782,220	Not available
ASEAN as % regular labour migrants	40.00%	99.78%	Not available

[a] Malaysia data is for 2018.

[b] Singapore migrant worker figure includes S passes (passes for mid-skilled workers, e.g., technicians) but excludes employment passes (available to professionals).

Source: Data compiled from Manpower Research and Statistics Department (2020); ILO (2019b, 2020b).

Lanka, Thailand and Vietnam. By contrast, Indonesian women could work in manufacturing, but Indonesian men could not (Immigration Department of Malaysia 2020a, 2020b). It is also significant that the number of labour migrants employed as domestic workers relative to the number employed in other sectors has decreased over time.

Singapore was the next destination country to develop a formal labour migration programme, accepting foreign workers to combat a labour shortage and rising wages (Chew and Chew 1989). Like Malaysia, it has long regulated the sectors in which foreigners can work and the countries from which they come. And, as in Malaysia, the rules governing eligible source countries have changed over time. As of 2020, workers from Malaysia, China, and 'North Asian Sources' (Hong Kong, Macau, South Korea, Taiwan) could be recruited in any of the six eligible sectors, while workers from 'Non-traditional Sources' (selected countries in South and South Asia) were eligible to work in all but manufacturing and services. Indonesians and Cambodians (and then only women) were only permitted to be employed as domestic workers. Within these different categories, workers of different national backgrounds could be recruited to specific sub-sectors, sometimes for different total lengths of time. Although Singapore does not make statistics by nationality publicly available, the inclusion of Northeast Asia as a source region for everything from domestic work to services is clearly driven more by Singapore's decision to open its doors to mainland Chinese than by any real expectation that large numbers of people from, say Taiwan or South Korea – if, indeed, any – will be recruited in these categories.

It was a long time before Thailand began to regulate inward labour migration, first establishing a retrospective system of registration allowing irregular migrants from Myanmar already living inside its borders to obtain employment in 1992, a scheme it later expanded to other nationalities (Ford 2019). However, it was not until the early 2000s that it began signing bilateral agreements sanctioning inward labour migration with Laos, Cambodia and Myanmar, and not until 2006 that it began operationalising them (Natali et al. 2014). A fourth bilateral agreement was later signed with Vietnam. As of 2020, there were 2,788,316 documented labour migrants in Thailand, registered under one of three different schemes, namely the bilateral Memorandum of Understanding (MOU), the post-arrival nationality verification scheme, or a smaller scheme for border employment. As a proportion of registered migrant workers, the number entering under the bilateral agreements – the scheme most like those used in other Asian destination countries – has risen dramatically over time. As of 2012, just 81,426 of Thailand's 1.85 million registered migrant workers had entered legally under a bilateral agreement (Thai Ministry of Labor cited in Hall 2012). In 2014, the number of participants rose to over a quarter of a million (ILO 2015), a number that almost quadrupled by 2019 (ILO 2020b).

Temporary labour migration is very gendered. In Singapore, the only occupation that is specifically assigned to men or women is domestic work, for which only women can be employed. However, many of the other sectors that are open to foreign workers – construction, shipyards, and petroleum and chemicals – are traditionally male-dominated. In practical terms, this means that women from Indonesia and Cambodia are permitted to work in Singapore (as domestic workers) but men from those countries cannot. In Malaysia, men accounted for 79 per cent of all regular migrant workers in 2018, but just 63 per cent of those from within Southeast Asia. Within the ASEAN cohort, the proportion of men ranged between 82 per cent of regular labour migrants from Myanmar to just 23 per cent from Cambodia. These disparities can be attributed to several factors. First, it may be related to the nature of the sector. For example, while there are no restrictions on who can be employed in the construction industry, the industry employs many more men than women. In the case of domestic workers, social assumptions about the gendered nature of work are reinforced through regulation. But these aspects of work can also intersect with other restrictions. The fact that Malaysia restricts country of origin to selected countries for domestic workers helps explain both the low numbers of women labour migrants from Myanmar and the relatively high number from Cambodia.

The number of women who migrate for work from a particular country of origin can also be influenced by that country's own policies. For example, the

Indonesian, Philippines and Cambodian governments have all imposed moratoria on travel to Malaysia at different times in response to reports of widespread abuse of domestic workers (Crinis and Bandali 2017). In Indonesia's case, the government imposed a ban on Malaysia from 2009 to 2011, and on Saudi Arabia from 2011 (Elias and Louth 2016). Then, in 2012, it announced a 'zero migrant domestic worker policy', which aimed to end the number of low-skilled women working abroad and increase their presence in higher-skill jobs, for example as care and health workers (Bachtiar and Tirtosudarmo 2017). The proportion of women leaving through government programmes dropped steadily from 2009, when women accounted for 83 per cent of labour migrants placed overseas, to 54 per cent in 2013, before rising again to 70 per cent by 2018 (BNP2TKI 2014, 2019). As this suggests, the government's aspirations to move to higher skilled migration foundered. By 2016, numbers of domestic workers had dropped markedly to a little more than one-sixth of their 2011 levels, but then doubled in 2017 (BNP2TKI 2014, 2019). Moreover, almost all the occupations in which both men and women were placed through the programme that year remained at the bottom of the skills continuum.

The management of temporary labour migration is highly politicised. As Clark and Pietsch (2014, 181) note, 'the migrant worker issue, more than any other, has negatively affected the relationship between the citizens and governments' of Indonesia and Malaysia. In the case of Singapore, the exclusion of Indonesians from migrating for any form of work beyond domestic labour is a clearly political decision, especially given that the lingua franca in many low-paying occupations in Singapore is Malay, a language closely related to Indonesian. At other times, Malaysia and Singapore have adjusted country-based quotas in response to tensions in a bilateral relationship or the 'poor' behaviour of a particular group of migrants (Ford 2019). For example, in 2002, Malaysia's deputy prime minister threatened to put an end to Indonesian labour migration after Indonesian workers rioted in an industrial zone in Negeri Sembilan. The government subsequently put a 'hire Indonesians last' policy in place (Ford 2006). A decade later, the Singaporean government deported twenty-nine migrant Chinese bus drivers and sentenced four more to imprisonment for taking strike action. The following year, hundreds of South Asian migrant workers were repatriated for failing to heed police orders to disperse when protesting against the lack of justice for 33-year-old construction worker was run over by a bus (Neo 2015).[18]

[18] Governments further afield have also adjusted their labour migration policies to punish their counterparts for perceived slights. For example, the Taiwanese government refused entry to migrants from various Southeast Asian countries, including workers from Thailand when the Thai government refused to issue a visa to the Taiwanese Minister of Labour (Ford 2019).

Country of origin governments react most strongly in response to incidents where female labour migrants have been abused. For example, the Philippines government halted labour exports to Singapore after the execution of a Filipina domestic worker there in the mid-1990s.[19] Over a decade later, the governments of first Indonesia and then Cambodia banned women from taking up employment as domestic workers in Malaysia, causing serious tensions in their relationship with the Malaysian government (Elias and Louth 2016). Female labour migrants have also been the primary focus for the public and advocacy groups in the Philippines and Indonesia, even though many men also migrate for work. In the Philippines, activists focus on female labour migrants, who they consider to be modern-day heroes and martyrs (Parreñas 2005). In Indonesia, public debate about labour migration has been dominated by narratives about female overseas workers, in which they have almost always been imagined as passive, good women at risk of commodification and sexualisation (Ford 2003). More recently, activists in both countries of origin and key destination countries in East and Southeast Asia have broadened their focus to include male temporary labour migrants (Ford 2019). However, both policymakers and activists continue to view and treat male and female labour migrants very differently.

4.3 Spontaneous Economic Migrants

In addition to asylum seekers and temporary labour migrants, Southeast Asia's border-crossers include spontaneous economic migrants: those who cross borders for economic reasons, but who do not fit government criteria for temporary labour migration. The first group of spontaneous economic migrants come through regular labour migration channels but either overstay or lose their right to work. Others have papers that appear to be legitimate but in fact are not. For example, many in Indonesia pass into Malaysia or Singapore with real passports obtained with fake documents, known to Indonesians as 'real but fake' (*asli tapi palsu, aspal*) (Ford and Lyons 2011).

Nengsih was one of those Indonesians who travelled the *aspal* route (cf. Ford and Lyons 2011). Nengsih had been employed in Singapore as a domestic worker while holding an *aspal* passport, eventually fell afoul of the law. When her first employer in Singapore treated her badly, she asked her agent to arrange a new placement. Concerned that the second employer was no better, she decided to run away. Not long after she returned to Batam, her agent – who did not have a licence – was raided by the police. Instead of returning to Java, as instructed by the authorities, she obtained a new passport under a different

[19] For details of the Flor Contemplacion case and its aftermath, see Hilsdon (2000) and Rodriguez (2010).

name, which she used for two years to travel in and out of Singapore, trading second-hand goods. Her luck ran out and she was detained at an immigration checkpoint. Once her immigration history was uncovered, she was tried and convicted, spending two and a half months in prison before being deported to Batam. When I interviewed her in Tanjung Pinang, she was planning to lie low for a few months before securing another *aspal* passport and trying her luck in Malaysia, where millions of Indonesians make their living without the right papers.

The profile of spontaneous economic migrants in Thailand – where they account for up to 10 per cent of the workforce (Bylander and Reid 2017) – is much more mixed. Undocumented workers from Cambodia, Laos and Myanmar, even some from China, are found in a broad cross-section of occupations in the formal and informal economy. While some of these workers are spontaneous economic migrants, many from Myanmar in particular meet the UNHCR's definition of 'refugee-like', even if they are not officially refugees. As I noted earlier, many asylum seekers eke out an existence in the informal economy in Thailand and Malaysia. However, some manage to find work in the formal economy. When I was researching irregular labour migration in 2007, a Burmese man cleaning my hotel room noticed documents from the UNHCR on my desk. His eyes lit up, and he asked me if I could help him secure refugee status. He had fled Myanmar several years earlier and, despite being undocumented, had managed to secure a relatively stable formal-sector job.

Conversely, some spontaneous economic migrants try to 'pass' as refugees. On the same research trip, I went for a massage in a shopping centre in Kuala Lumpur. The masseuse was a middle-aged Acehnese woman who had lived in Medan since childhood, and who had entered Malaysia on a visitor's pass in 2002. Although a university graduate, she decided to stay, and found work at the massage shop. When the Malaysian government began issuing temporary residence permits to Acehnese after the 2004 tsunami, she decided to try her luck. Upon making enquiries, she discovered that she would have to pass an Acehnese language test to be eligible. Her Acehnese was quite poor, but she passed the test – unlike several Javanese, who had applied at the same time, hoping to convince Malaysian authorities that they too were from Aceh (Ford 2007).

As both these examples suggest – despite the complex systems established by countries of origin to manage temporary labour migration – the burden of border policing falls largely on the shoulders of region's destination countries. Southeast Asia's three destination countries differ in the way that they police irregularity. Under Singapore's Foreign Manpower Employment Act of 2012, employers were held responsible for ensuring that foreign workers do not engage in 'illegal, immoral or undesirable conduct', and for the cost of repatriation, should a work pass be cancelled or revoked. It also required that employers notify the Controller within seven days if a foreign worker went missing, and within twelve hours of the employer becoming aware of their death. Employers risked fines of up to SGD 10,000 if they fail to comply (Singapore Government 2012).

By contrast, Malaysia does little to attempt to control irregular migrants while in-country. Instead, it has used periodic mass deportations, interspersed with sporadic amnesty programmes that allow irregular migrant workers to legalise their status, to manage them (Ford 2019). The most confronting of these mass deportations was the Nunukan Affair (Ford 2006). After the Malaysian government implemented a new Immigration Act on 1 August 2002, it forcibly repatriated some 140,000 Indonesians to the island of Nunukan, just over the border from the eastern state of Sabah. This massive repatriation followed on the heels of a two-month amnesty for undocumented workers, during which a similar number of Indonesians had returned home. As a consequence, Nunukan's population was already much higher than normal when the repatriations began. Most of the undocumented workers were directly shipped to other places in Indonesia. But some 40,000 people remained either in a camp administered by a registered labour sending company or in the community. Many among them fell sick, and some seventy died (Palupi and Yasser 2002). Local residents were also severely affected by the inability of the town's infrastructure to cope with the four-fold increase in population, and sharp rises in the price of basic commodities.

Although Thailand has generally favoured regularisation, it has also resorted to more punitive measures, including deportation (Hedman 2008). According to statistics released by the governments of Cambodia, Laos and Myanmar, over 300,000 migrant workers returned from Thailand between March and June 2020 (ILO 2020a). Thai authorities began deporting more workers as the number of COVID-19 cases began to rise. In the first few weeks of 2021, over 35,000 more Cambodians were sent home (*BenarNews* 2021). During that same period, however, the Thai government also implemented a regularisation programme in an attempt to curb the spread of the virus among workers (Richardson and Pettigrew 2022).

The cost of policing borders is certainly one factor in states' responses to this group of border-crossers. While it is relatively easy for Singapore to maintain high levels of border surveillance, Thailand's and Malaysia's long land and sea borders are relatively easily traversed. Importantly, however, the porousness of borders does not always explain their sustained presence. As the International Labour Organization (ILO) acknowledges, governments tolerate spontaneous economic migrants for a range of reasons, including 'the usefulness of migrants for certain interest groups' (ILO 2010, 33). The most obvious interest group is of course employers, who benefit from a workforce that cannot access the formal protections available to regular workers and that cannot afford to draw attention to their presence. However, the broader community also benefits from the presence of this especially cheap, pliable workforce.

4.4 Victims of Trafficking?

The border-crossing experiences of spontaneous economic migrants vary greatly. Many who cross land borders, or even some of the region's sea borders, are able to enter into a neighbouring country in a matter of minutes. Others travel thousands of kilometres, risking life and limb, with a people smuggler. It is this cohort that is most often targeted in campaigns against people smuggling and human trafficking. There is no doubt that men and women who cross Southeast Asian borders for political or economic reasons take risks, including of being exploited by people smugglers or deceived or coerced by human traffickers. For example, most workers in Thailand's fishing industry are migrants from Cambodia, Laos and Myanmar who originally engaged brokers and human smugglers to enter Thailand. Upon arrival the conditions in which they were required to work were very different from those promised to them (HRW 2018). However, many more border-crossers are now branded as victims of trafficking with little consideration of their positionality, needs or agency (e.g., Eilenberg 2012; Molland 2012).

The rise of the anti-trafficking frame has affected the experiences of asylum seekers and refugees. In some cases, asylum seekers have benefited from being categorised as victims of trafficking. For example, in the early 2010s, it became common for Afghans to be detained at Kuala Lumpur International Airport on the suspicion that they had been trafficked (Lyons and Ford 2014). Malaysian law does not recognise asylum seekers, and the Immigration Act stipulates that migrants who enter without documentation can be given a substantial fine, imprisoned for up to five years or even caned, before being deported. However, under the 2007 anti-trafficking law, persons found to be genuine victims of trafficking are placed in a shelter for up to three months before being returned to their country of origin. This form of temporary protection is significantly less than the protection required under the Refugee Convention but it is considerably better than the treatment received by most undocumented arrivals.

Anti-trafficking measures have had implications, for example, for Rohingya seeking assistance from people smugglers to enter Malaysia. In one such case, several hundred people were detained for a prolonged period in what have been described as 'trafficking camps' close to the Thai-Malaysian border (UNODC 2017). In May 2015, a joint military-police taskforce in Thailand found at least thirty Rohingya bodies at one such camp (HRW 2015). When news of the graves became public, commentators were quick to represent the situation as a case of asylum seekers who had become victims of trafficking (Mutaqin 2018). The mass graves attracted sufficient attention that the Thai government decided to crack down on illegal migration networks (Grewcock 2018). It also moved to prosecute more than sixty defendants, including a former army Lieutenant General, who were found guilty of several charges, including human trafficking and smuggling (Reuters, 1 November 2019).[20] But even where individuals are prosecuted – as in both these cases – the anti-trafficking approach does nothing to address the underlying causes of the refugee crisis. There is even a risk that asylum seekers identified as victims of trafficking may be robbed of the opportunity to gain official refugee status and instead be repatriated to the very country where they experienced persecution.

Temporary labour migrants, and especially women, have also become caught up in anti-trafficking efforts. From the early 2000s, US-funded anti-trafficking programmes transformed the activist landscape in Indonesia's Riau Islands (Ford and Lyons 2012b). In 2001, there were no non-governmental organisations (NGOs) working on human trafficking or international labour migration in Tanjung Pinang. According to one NGO activist, by 2006 the city had been engulfed in 'the anti-trafficking fever' (Interview, November 2009). As another NGO activist observed, 'Suddenly there were so many NGOs dealing with trafficking. It was like a magnet. Everyone's attention shifted. Everyone wanted to work on it. The ones that used to deal with other issues all shifted focus and a whole bunch of new ones emerged' (Interview, November 2006). Reflecting the emerging focus on labour trafficking in this period, the primary focus of these programmes was on temporary labour migrants. As a third activist observed:

> In Tanjung Pinang, trafficking is synonymous with migrant workers. Migrant workers aren't trafficked if they are fully aware of what they're getting into; have full control over their circumstances; know exactly where they're going, what they'll be doing and how much they'll get paid; and can work without any kind of pressure. But no-one's really in that kind of situation. They're trapped in an illusion that all their economic woes will be solved if they can get work and so they pay an illegal passport agent and go overseas. That's

[20] Police made nine arrests in another case in Malaysia, among them five immigration officials who were allegedly involved with a trafficking syndicate selling Rohingya into forced labour (ERT 2010).

> why smuggling is also really a form of trafficking. If workers really know what they're doing, they'll go through legal channels. But even then, there's a chance that they'll be trafficked, because the agents promise more than they'll deliver. That's the great irony of it – the government is also a trafficker. (Interview, November 2006)

Desperate to improve conditions for labour migrants, advocates in many parts of Southeast Asia have turned to anti-trafficking laws because they feel that labour laws have been ineffective. For example, when Malaysia passed its anti-trafficking law in 2007, migrant rights organisations in that country decided to use it to argue for criminal prosecution of forced labour cases in a context where labour legislation had failed (Lyons and Ford 2014). While this approach produced some short-term gains for some temporary labour migrants, it did little to address the system-wide factors that create and sustain their endemic abuse. As Shamir (2012) has observed, the anti-trafficking frame positions labour migrants as passive victims to be extracted from harmful work environments rather than dealing with the economic, social and legal conditions that make them vulnerable to exploitation.

The group least likely to be truly victims of trafficking yet most likely to be caught up in anti-trafficking measures are members of borderlands communities themselves. Borderlanders making routine border crossings are easy fodder for officials seeking to prove their anti-trafficking credentials. For example, people living along Indonesia's land border with Malaysia regularly cross it illegally – often with the assistance of other members of the borderlands community – in order to avoid the long bureaucratic process involved in obtaining the documentation required to seek work in Sarawak. Local authorities turned a blind eye to these illegal border-crossers until the governments of Indonesia and Malaysia began treating undocumented labour migration as organised human trafficking. Borderlanders were labelled as victims of trafficking, while those who facilitated their border-crossing were increasingly harassed, fined, or even arrested as traffickers or people smugglers (Eilenberg 2012).

The group of spontaneous economic migrants most affected by the anti-trafficking push are migrant sex workers, the majority of whom are women. In Singapore – where most sex workers come from Thailand, Philippines, Indonesia, Vietnam and China – brothel-based sex work operates under a Medical Surveillance Scheme while other forms of sex work are technically illegal (Wong et al. 2012). This changed in 2012, when the United States Trafficking in Persons (TIP) process pushed Singapore to take steps to reduce the demand for sex work, and the police began to regularly raid brothels. Although they reportedly only arrested pimps, this change in policy contributed to a climate of fear in the sex industry and threatened the well-being of women working in it (Chapman-Schmidt 2015).[21] In other cases, governments pay lip-service to the anti-trafficking agenda while continuing to allow cross-border activity that may in fact involve risks of trafficking. For example, China has responded to efforts by international actors to address human trafficking, but it still permits Vietnamese women to cross the border without documentation to sell sex in the city of Hekou (Zhang 2012). These women are allowed to work indefinitely without documents because the local government benefits from the town's reputation as a sex tourism destination.

As Lindquist (2010) argues, the human trafficking approach 'has a depoliticizing function through the concern with – and intervention on behalf of – a particular type of migrant . . . rather than broader issues such as labor rights and the freedom of mobility'. Also striking is the emphasis within this frame on border protection over victims' rights. All Southeast Asian source countries have taken steps to criminalise human trafficking. But relatively few trafficking cases are investigated or prosecuted, and those that are overwhelmingly involve sex trafficking. By the late 2010s, the Philippine authorities were investigating about 400 trafficking cases a year, leading to 200 or so prosecutions annually, primarily for sex trafficking offences (US Department of State 2019). Similarly, Myanmar reported investigating about 200 trafficking cases per year in 2017 and 2018, the vast majority of which involved cases of forced marriage to Chinese men. Over 500 individuals were convicted of sex trafficking in 2017, with most trials being conducted in absentia (US Department of State 2019).

The situation is much the same in destination countries, where even though these countries host hundreds of thousands of migrants who could be considered to be victims of trafficking, laws that criminalise trafficking are seldom used. In Singapore, 80 per cent of human trafficking cases investigated in 2013 involved female minors in the sex industry (Yea 2015). In 2018, the government only investigated sixteen cases, the majority of which involved sex trafficking (US Department of State 2019). And, despite known cases of serious abuse, including sexual abuse, no cases of forced domestic servitude have ever been prosecuted in Singapore. As this suggests, the primary purpose of anti-trafficking measures is to control border-crossers rather than to protect victims of trafficking.

5 Impact on Host Communities

Cross-border mobility and attempts to prevent it are highly political acts with implications not only for the individual border-crossers but for host communities.

[21] Anti-trafficking frames have also been used in Cambodia and Indonesia to deal with internal migrants who become involved in sex work. For details see Lyons and Ford (2010) and Sandy (2012).

For many Singaporeans, borders work to reinforce national identity, based on a strong sense of nationalist exceptionalism as Southeast Asia's 'little red dot' – a reference to Singapore's Chinese identity in a sea of Malays. Similarly, the presence of refugees and spontaneous economic migrants from Myanmar in Thailand more often serve to inscribe difference than encourage integration. The presence of a foreign underclass brings economic benefits but also too often a deep sense of unease, which is both exacerbated and domesticated by a process of othering. At the same time – just as the presence of foreign workers alleviates the need to restructure unequal economies – the presence of large number of foreign women, be they workers or marriage migrants, makes it possible to postpone hard discussions about gender roles at home.

5.1 A Foreign Underclass

Destination countries clearly benefit from the presence of foreign workers, be they there legally or illegally. Temporary labour migration through formal channels is attractive to destination country governments because of its inherent flexibility, and thus its capacity to respond to changes in the economic or political climate. Spontaneous economic migrants are more difficult to get rid of, but it is abundantly clear that destination countries also benefit from their presence. For example, following the Asian Financial Crisis of 1997–98, the Thai government encouraged foreign-owned factories producing clothing and footwear for export to move their operations from Bangkok into the provinces along the Burmese border to take advantage of cheap Burmese labour (Chalamwong 2004).

Importantly, also, the presence of a large foreign workforce makes it possible for destination country governments to avoid dealing with structural inequalities. In addition, countries of origin bear the costs of social reproduction, as well as the social and economic costs of supporting returned migrant workers who have been in some way traumatised, or who have spent all their economically productive years abroad. In the workplace, moreover, the impetus to question the basis of overly large gaps between high-paid and low-paid occupations – and to improve occupational health and safety in dirty or dangerous industries – simply disappears when low-paid occupations are filled by foreigners. Ironically, citizens of those destination countries often do not even recognise the evident economic contribution of these foreign workers. The majority of respondents to a 2010 ILO survey were unhappy about the presence of migrant workers. A follow-up survey conducted in 2019 by the ILO and UN Women revealed that 47 per cent of Malaysians, 40 per cent of Thais and 30 per cent of Singaporeans believed that migrant workers were a drain on the economy

(ILO 2019a). At times, concerns about the influence of these foreign workers on the opportunities for local workers are strong enough to influence government policy. For example, the Singaporean government responded to public frustration in 2007 by cracking down on employers' attempts to increase their quota of foreign workers by pretending to hire more local workers (Ong 2014).

The calculus around asylum seekers and refugees is more complicated, and both Thailand and Malaysia have struggled with demands of managing their presence. But they certainly constitute another important element of these countries' foreign underclass: some refugees are ultimately resettled, but many others remain in Thailand or Malaysia for decades, if not permanently. The lives of residents in Thailand's border camps are governed by camp authorities, and they face restrictions on their mobility. In some camps, refugees are allowed to leave for work or other purposes (Banki and Lang 2008, 67). In others, any refugees found outside the camp's perimeter are detained and sent back to Myanmar (Interview with Jesuit Refugee Service Representative, February 2007).

In Malaysia, asylum seekers survive in squatter settlements on the urban fringe or even in the jungle unless they are being held in immigration detention alongside irregular migrant workers (Wong and Anwar 2003).[22] There, they live in fear of the police and immigration officials, but also members of RELA (Jabatan Sukarelawan Malaysia), an organisation of 'volunteers' who are paid a bounty for each undocumented person they apprehend. As few refugees have work permits, they also risk being detained, fined or caned if their workplace is raided (Interviews with NGO activists, February 2007). With no prospect of local settlement, or even permission to legally engage in paid employment, they eke out a living at the edges of the economy, often relying on support from community organisations to survive.

5.2 The Process of Othering

Destination countries benefit economically from the presence of temporary labour migrants and spontaneous economic migrants. But their presence, and the presence of asylum seekers and refugees, is by no means politically or socially neutral. The ILO survey cited above found that 68 per cent of Malaysians, 58 per cent of Thais and 53 per cent of Singaporeans felt that migrant workers threaten their culture and heritage (ILO 2019a). These statistics ring true with what I was told in the field. When I was conducting fieldwork on refugees and spontaneous economic migration in Thailand in 2007, Thais

[22] For more details of refugees' living conditions in Malaysia, see Hoffstaedter (2014, 2015).

and Burmese alike described the deep community hostility towards Burmese living in Thailand. It was also evident that Thai informants were not as negative towards economic migrants from Laos, who not only blended in more physically but also had a better command of the Thai language. In Malaysia, however, the fact that Indonesians are culturally and linguistically similar to the Malays does not save them from discrimination, not least because many Malays view them as being chaotic and lax in their practice of Islam.

But being a devout Muslim is also not enough to guarantee acceptance in Malaysia. One of the reasons that many Rohingya make their way to Malaysia rather than staying in Thailand is that Malaysia is a Muslim country (Azis 2014). Indeed, one Rohingya man told Azis that he had imagined Malaysia would be 'heaven', in 'contrast to the hell of Myanmar'. But the reality of life in Malaysia proved crushingly different. Many of his compatriots, who had also imagined Malaysia as a 'Muslim city of refuge', subsequently became disillusioned by what they saw as Malaysians' half-hearted religiosity and lack of solidarity with their fellow Muslims. In fact, many who had spent an extended time in transit observed that Thailand had been more hospitable (Azis 2014, 841–2).

There are also repeated moral panics about the impact of foreign workers' presence on local communities (Crinis 2005; Killias 2014). While there is no real evidence to suggest that migrant workers commit more crimes than the rest of the population, 72 per cent of Thais and 59 per cent of Malaysians responding to the ILO survey were convinced that they did (ILO 2019a). When I was doing fieldwork in Malaysia in 2007, I encountered a West Sumatran taxi-driver who had held permanent residency status since 1979. There were many things he liked about living in Malaysia, but he felt constantly attacked for being Indonesian. As he told me, 'The Malaysians never stop criticising us. They go on and on and on. If you listened to them, you'd think that Indonesians were responsible for every single thing that ever went wrong in Malaysia.' This assessment is not surprising. Reports in the late 1980s highlighted Indonesian migrants' involvement in drug-trafficking, burglary involving the use of black magic and kidnappings (Ford 2006), while Crinis' (2004) survey of English-language Malaysian newspapers in the early 2000s revealed a strong focus on the social problems associated with migrants, including disease, drug use, violence, murder and rape.

Xenophobic attitudes are always present, but they hit a new high during the COVID-19 pandemic. As in many other parts of the world, the citizens of Southeast Asia's destination countries were deeply concerned about the prospect of migrant workers spreading the virus. In Singapore, for example, a survey using the COVID-19 Quality of Life Scale administered in late 2020 and early 2021 found that Singaporeans' biggest fear during that period was that the virus would be spread by foreigners (Ang and Das 2022). There is no doubt that migrant workers were blamed by many for the spread of COVID-19 (Boris 2022; Dewanto 2020). The increasing number of cases in migrant worker dormitories early on during the pandemic prompted 'racist statements' and 'stereotypical portrayals' of migrant workers in the mainstream media, describing the countries from which they come from 'backward' and attacking them personally for their 'poor hygiene' (Ang and Das 2022, 8) whilst failing to take the dormitories' cramped conditions into account (Hamid 2021).

Governments in the region respond to such moral panics by imposing different kinds of controls on migrant workers, a fact nowhere clearer than in the Singaporean government's response to the COVID-19 pandemic. As discussed earlier, Singapore subjected regular temporary labour migrants to onerous controls on their working and living environments even before the advent of COVID-19. Then, on 5 April 2020, it locked down two migrant worker dormitories with large numbers of confirmed COVID-19 cases. Two days later, all dormitories – accommodating some 300,000 migrant workers – were locked down when general stay-at-home orders were issued (Han 2020; Wong and Zhou 2020). Even after it relaxed arrangements later in 2020, migrant workers were only permitted to leave the dormitories for four hours on their days off, and then only to designated recreation centres (Chattoraj 2022).

5.3 Preserving Gender Norms

In host communities, cheap domestic labour also frees middle-class women from their household duties, allowing them to engage in paid work without governments having to increase investment in social infrastructure (Crinis and Bandali 2017; Hill, Baird and Ford 2017; Lyons 2017). Care work is considered 'a natural expression and outcome of women's reproductive and nurturing roles and capacities' in destination countries like Singapore (Lyons 2017, 55). But the responsibilities that come with it are parsed by class and ethnicity. Unable to rely on government-funded services, working-class women – and particularly those of non-Chinese ethnicity – are largely expected to forego paid work to care for children and the elderly, thereby making way for working-class men. On the other hand, their middle- and upper-class counterparts are expected to carry the mental and emotional burden of care work, but most of the physical labour associated with it is done by foreign domestic workers (Lyons 2017). Consequently, both male and female employers end up perpetuating gendered notions about the reproductive sphere by reallocating household responsibilities from local to migrant women (Huang and Yeoh 1998).

Many foreign marriages also serve to prop up patriarchal family norms. As Piper (2006) observes, men and women are affected differently by political change, laws or migration policies, as well as by policies that determine the extent of their integration within host countries. In Malaysia, it is easier for foreign husbands of Malaysian citizens to secure a work permit than a foreign wife (Leng, Yeoh and Shuib 2012). In Singapore, meanwhile, immigration authorities will only grant permanent residence to the foreign husband of a Singaporean woman if he is gainfully employed. By contrast, foreign wives of Singaporean men are only eligible for residency if their husbands can demonstrate that they have the financial means to support them (Lyons and Ford 2008). These norms feed into practices in many households. In the Singaporean case, most marriages to foreigners involve economically marginalised men seeking 'traditional' wives. As one Thai woman told Jongwilaiwan and Thompson (2013, 369), 'You know, a husband does not have to hire a maid because Thai women can do everything.' In Malaysia, too, foreign wives tend to make an outsize contribution to reproductive labour, especially with regard to the care of the elderly (Lumayag 2016).

As in a number of East Asian countries, the presence of foreign wives raises concerns about their inability to fit into the host society. Zhang and Yeoh (2020, 1415–16) report that, in Singapore, there is 'widespread public speculation and suspicion' about the economic motivations of marriage migrants, and concerns that gaps in age, language barriers and cultural and socio-economic differences are too great to overcome. In Malaysia, official statistics suggest that around half of foreign wives come from Indonesia or India, countries that share similar cultures to two of Malaysia's three main ethnic groups (Lumayag 2016). However, these cultural similarities may mask many differences in daily practices or expectations. The gap is of course greater when marriage migrants come from different cultural backgrounds. For example, Jongwilaiwan and Thompson (2013, 375) describe different 'culturally laden conflicts' between Thai wives and their Singaporean families, 'frequently tinged with ethnic and class-based prejudices'. There are also widely held doubts that foreign wives are capable of nurturing the next generation, paralleling concerns – sometimes bordering on moral panic – about trusting children to the care of foreign domestic workers (Yeoh et al. 1999).

Of course, temporary labour migration also has complex implications for the gender orders not only of host communities, but also communities of origin. When men leave for long periods of time, women may experience greater autonomy in the household. If they receive remittances from partners working overseas, they may have more resources and greater control over household decision-making than they would have if their partners stayed at home. When women leave, they create transnational 'care chains' (cf. Hochschild 2000), whereby their own children must be cared for by others while they engage in reproductive labour in wealthier countries. Most enlist the help of their female relatives to care for their children but there are also shifts in the gendered practices of care, with many fathers left behind taking on some care work. However, this seldom disrupts gendered ideologies about parenthood and childcare – in the Philippines, for example, many left-behind father-carers say they would have rather migrated themselves than taking on 'female' roles (Lam and Yeoh 2018).

Women's capacity to generate economic resources through work overseas can also lead to a renegotiation of power relations within the household, as evidenced by Indonesian women's experiences.[23] Some women may choose to work abroad through a sense of adventure or to escape a bad relationship, though most see overseas domestic work as a way of obtaining the financial security they need to feed, house and educate their children, and perhaps build a nicer house or establish a small business (Ford 2001, 2003). Regardless of their motivations, women's experience abroad mean that many are confronted by the narrow confines of their village lives upon their return (von der Borch 2008; Nurchayati 2017). For some women, enhanced financial power, and lived experience, changes the power dynamics in their household. One returned migrant interviewed by Nurchayati (2017), for example, encouraged her husband to take responsibility for the family's washing. When he did so, the women in his family berated him for letting her embarrass him (and them). When forced to choose between his wife and his family, he chose to accept his wife's new expectations in regard to the division of household labour. In other cases, women may return to discover that their husbands have entered new relationships, leaving them to forge a new life, or to migrate again.

6 Conclusion

Southeast Asia has always been – and will always be – shaped by cross-border mobility. At different intervals, people have fled *en masse* from Cambodia, Indonesia, Laos, Myanmar, the Philippines, Thailand, Timor-Leste and Vietnam to other countries within Southeast Asia and beyond. Migration for economic advantage, including through marriage migration, is also

[23] The overseas migration of married women with children also opens a labour market for local domestic workers (Lindio-McGovern 2017). While these local domestic workers may be very poorly paid, access to paid work potentially provides them with a pathway to economic independence (Hill et al. 2017).

a fundamental part of the region's past and present. In the past, many economic migrants relocated permanently but, as borders have hardened, overseas contract work has become the dominant form of labour migration, at least among those who use official channels to go abroad. As the preceding sections have demonstrated, it is impossible to draw a sharp line between asylum seekers and economic migrants or, indeed, between these groups and victims of trafficking. This fundamental truth is nowhere better illustrated than by the story of Nengsih, the woman who was arrested for working illegally in Singapore. At different times in her extended period of border-crossing, Nengsih could be considered a regular labour migrant (her passport was real, after all, even though it was fake), a smuggled person or victim of trafficking. Later, she became a smuggler, though of goods not of people.

Ultimately, outcomes matter far more to border-crossers than what label is applied to them (McAdam 2018). However, the nuances are important. For example, using the trafficking yardstick, with its emphasis on human tragedy, to measure labour exploitation has two possible outcomes. On the one hand, it can mean that less serious violations of foreign workers' labour rights may be deemed unworthy of attention. On the other hand, it can lead to bloated claims about those same labour rights violations; for example, that underpayment of wages equates to modern slavery. Neither response is likely to lead to satisfactory redress. At best, the underpaid labour migrant struggles on in exploitative conditions. At worst, s/he is identified as a victim of trafficking and involuntarily loses their opportunity to work abroad and with it their capacity to reach their financial goals or even to repay debt.

As this Element has emphasised, the decisions that governments make about how to categorise and manage different groups of border-crossers are highly political. Ultimately, domestic politics, and even international relations, drive the region's bordering regimes more than technocratic matters like border policing or labour market demand. Policies on permanent migration to Singapore and Malaysia are influenced by concerns about maintaining an 'ideal' racial balance. In Indonesia, professionals and factory workers alike fear that they will not be able to compete should there be an influx of foreigners (Field observations, various years). At times, destination countries have favoured employer demand over anti-migrant sentiment. At others, they have made adjustments to their policies in response to tensions in a bilateral relationship or the 'poor' behaviour of a particular group of migrants. These considerations are apparent in Thailand's periodic attempts to work with Myanmar to facilitate the repatriation of asylum seekers and Malaysia's relative openness to Muslim asylum seekers, but also in both countries' refusal to sign the Refugee Convention. The politics of the anti-trafficking agenda is even more apparent in countries' rush to pass anti-trafficking laws, but also in their reluctance to enforce them.

Such is the magnitude and frequency of border-crossing in all its manifestations that it simply cannot be ignored when studying Southeast Asia. But it is also of vital importance when studying individual Southeast Asian countries. Historical mobility into and within the region have made all these countries what they are today, enriching their cultures, shaping their sense of identity, and even their institutions. Borderlands communities throughout the region continue to be influenced as much – sometimes more – by communities across the border as they are by their fellow citizens, or even their own government. Whole countries, and especially the migrant-sending communities within them, are affected by the experiences of the men and women who leave even temporarily. The social and political impact of large-scale border-crossing is most evident, however, in the countries to which these people travel. It is in fact impossible to understand the social and political dynamics in Singapore, Malaysia or Thailand without considering the foreigners who live and work there. The challenge is, then, to develop models that better take into account these mobile populations when understanding individual countries as well as Southeast Asia as a whole.

References

ADB, ILO and OECD. 2016. *Labor Migration in Asia: Building Effective Institutions*. Tokyo: ADBI.

Amer, Ramses and Keyuan Zou. 2011. *Conflict Management and Dispute Settlement in East Asia*. Farnham: Ashgate.

Anderson, Benedict. 2007. 'The Idea of Power in Javanese Culture'. In *Culture and Politics in Indonesia*, edited by Claire Holt, 1–70. Jakarta: Equinox.

Ang, Chin-Siang and Arul Das. 2022. 'Dirty Foreigners' Are to Blame for COVID-19: Impacts of COVID Stress Syndrome on Quality of Life and Gratitude among Singaporean Adults. *Current Psychology*. https://doi.org/10.1007/s12144-021-02560-3.

Angenendt, Steffen and Anne Koch. 2017. *Global Migration Governance and Mixed Flows*. Berlin: Stiftung Wissenschaft und Politik.

Azis, Avyanthi. 2014. 'Urban Refugees in a Graduated Sovereignty: The Experiences of the Stateless Rohingya in the Klang Valley'. *Citizenship Studies* 18 (8): 839–54.

Bachtiar, Palmira and Riwanto Tirtosudarmo. 2017. 'From Domestic Workers to Care Workers, Understanding the Dynamics of Indonesia's Overseas Labour Mobility'. *Asia Pacific Journal of Social Work and Development* 27 (3): 142–58.

Banki, Susan and Hazel Lang. 2008. 'Protracted Displacement on the Thai–Burmese Border: The Interrelated Search for Durable Solutions'. In *Protracted Displacement in Asia: No Place to Call*, edited by Howard Adelman, 59–81. Aldershot: Ashgate.

Betts, Alexander. 2011. *Protection by Persuasion: International Cooperation in the Refugee Regime*. Ithaca: Cornell University Press.

BNP2TKI. 2014. *Penempatan dan Perlindungan Tenaga Kerja Indonesia Tahun 2013*. Jakarta: BNP2TKI.

BNP2TKI. 2019. *Data Penempatan dan Perlindungan PMI Periode Tahun 2018*. Jakarta: BNP2TKI.

Boris, Eileen. 2022. 'Vulnerability and Resilience in the Covid-19 Crisis: Race, Gender, and Belonging'. In *Migration and Pandemics: Spaces of Solidarity and Spaces of Exception*, edited by Anna Triandafyllidou, 65–84. Switzerland: Springer.

Brees, Inge. 2010. 'Burden or Boon: The Impact of Burmese Refugees on Thailand'. *Whitehead Journal of Diplomacy and International Relations* 11 (1): 35–48.

Bylander, Maryann. 2016. *Cambodian Migration to Thailand: The Role of Environmental Shocks and Stress*. Washington, DC: World Bank.

Bylander, Maryann and Georgia Reid. 2017. *Criminalizing Irregular Migrant Labour: Thailand's Crackdown in Context*. Washington, DC: Migration Policy Institute.

Castles, Stephen. 2011. 'Migration, Crisis, and the Global Labour Market'. *Globalizations* 8 (3): 311–24.

Chalamwong, Yongyuth. 2004. 'Government Policies on International Migration: Illegal Workers in Thailand'. In *International Migration in Southeast Asia*, edited by Aris Ananta and Evi Arifin. Singapore: Institute of Southeast Asian Studies.

Chantavanich, Supang. 2011. 'Cross-border Displaced Persons from Myanmar in Thailand'. In *Migration for Development in Thailand: Overview and Tools for Policymakers*, edited by Jerrold Huguet and Aphichat Chamratrithirong, 119–29. Bangkok: IOM.

Chapman-Schmidt, Ben. 2015. 'Sex in the Shadow of the Law: Regulating Sex Work and Human Trafficking in Singapore'. *Asian Journal of Comparative Law* 10: 1–21.

Chattoraj, Diotima. 2022. '"We Are All Migrant Workers": Commonality of Bangladeshi Migrants' Experiences in Singapore amidst Covid-19'. *International Journal of Asia-Pacific Studies* 18: 9–36.

Chew, Soon Beng and Rosalind Chew. 1989. 'Industrial Relations in Singapore'. *Singapore Economic Review* 34 (2): 47–63.

Clark, Marshall and Juliet Pietsch. 2014. *Indonesia–Malaysia Relations: Cultural Heritage, Politics and Labour Migration*. London: Routledge.

Crinis, Vicki. 2004. 'The Silence and Fantasy of Women and Work'. PhD Thesis, University of Wollongong.

Crinis, Vicki. 2005. 'The Devil You Know: Malaysian Perceptions of Foreign Workers'. *Review of Indonesian and Malaysian Affairs* 39 (2): 91–111.

Crinis, Vicki and Alifa Bandali. 2017. 'Malaysia: Balancing Paid and Unpaid Work'. In *Women, Work and Care in the Asia–Pacific*, edited by Marian Baird, Michele Ford and Elizabeth Hill, 41–54. Abingdon: Routledge.

Crisp, Jeff. 2008. *Beyond the Nexus: UNHCR's Evolving Perspective on Refugee Protection and International Migration*. Switzerland: UNHCR.

David, Roman and Ian Holliday. 2018. *Liberalism and Democracy in Myanmar*. Oxford: Oxford University Press.

Davies, Sara. 2008. *Legitimising Rejection: International Refugee Law in Southeast Asia*. Leiden: Martinus Nijhoff.

Decobert, Anne. 2016. *The Politics of Aid to Burma: A Humanitarian Struggle on the Thai–Burmese Border*. New York: Routledge.

Derks, Annuska. 2011. 'The Politics and Profits of "Labour Export"'. In *Cambodia's Economic Transformation*, edited by Caroline Hughes and Kheang Un, 182–98. Copenhagen: NIAS Press.

Dewanto, Pamungkas. 2020. *Labouring Situations and Protection among Foreign Workers in Malaysia*. Bangkok: Heinrich Boell Stiftung. https://th.boell.org/sites/default/files/grid/2020/10/12/NewOffice.jpg.

Eilenberg, Michael. 2012. 'Territorial Sovereignty and Trafficking in the Indonesia–Malaysia Borderlands'. In *Labour Migration and Human Trafficking in Southeast Asia: Critical Perspectives*, edited by Michele Ford, Lenore Lyons and Willem van Schendel, 112–29. London: Routledge.

Elias, Juanita and Jonathon Louth. 2016. 'Regional Dispute over the Transnationalization of Domestic Labour: Malaysia's "Maid Shortage" and Foreign Relations with Indonesia and Cambodia'. In *The Everyday Political Economy of Southeast Asia*, edited by Juanita Elias and Lena Rethel, 196–217. Cambridge: Cambridge University Press.

Elmhirst, Rebecca Carl Middleton and Bernadette P. Resurrección. 2017. 'Migration and Floods in Southeast Asia: A Mobile Political Ecology of Vulnerability, Resilience and Social Justice'. In *Living with Floods in a Mobile Southeast Asia: A Political Ecology of Vulnerability, Migration and Environmental Change*, edited by Middleton, Carl, Rebecca Elmhirst and Supang Chantavanich, 1–21. London: Routledge.

ERT. 2010. *Trapped in a Cycle of Flight: Stateless Rohingya in Malaysia*. London: The Equal Rights Trust.

ERT. 2014. *Equal Only in Name: The Human Rights of Stateless Rohingya in Malaysia*. London: The Equal Rights Trust and the Institute of Human Rights and Peace Studies.

Fadli. 2020a. Indonesia Asks Singapore to Reopen Borders as Bintan 'Ready to Receive Tourists'. *The Jakarta Post*, 3 July. www.thejakartapost.com/news/2020/07/03/indonesia-asks-singapore-to-reopen-borders-as-bintan-ready-to-receive-tourists.html.

Fadli. 2020b. Covid-19: Batam Ferry Terminal Mulls Suspending Operations amid Declining Income. *The Jakarta Post*, 18 March. www.thejakartapost.com/news/2020/03/18/covid-19-batam-ferry-terminal-mulls-suspending-operations-amid-declining-income.html

Fealy, Greg. 2019. 'Reformasi and the Decline of Liberal Islam'. *In Activists in Transition: Progressive Politics in Democratic Indonesia*, edited by Thushara Dibley and Michele Ford, 117–34. Ithaca: Cornell University Press.

FIDH and SUARAM. 2008. *Undocumented Migrants and Refugees in Malaysia: Raids, Detention and Discrimination*. Paris: Federation Internationale des Ligues des Droits de l'Homme.

Ford, Michele. 2001. 'Indonesian Women as Export Commodity: Notes from Tanjung Pinang'. *Labour and Management in Development* 2 (5): 1–9.

Ford, Michele. 2003. 'Beyond the Femina Fantasy: Female Industrial and Overseas Domestic Labour in Indonesian Discourses of Women's Work'. *Review of Indonesian and Malaysian Affairs* 37 (2): 83–113.

Ford, Michele. 2006. 'After Nunukan: The Regulation of Indonesian Migration to Malaysia'. In *Mobility, Labour Migration and Border Controls in Asia*, edited by Amarjit Kaur and Ian Metcalfe, 228–47. New York: Palgrave Macmillan.

Ford, Michele. 2007. *Advocacy Responses to Irregular Labour Migration in ASEAN: The Cases of Malaysia and Thailand*. Manila: MFA/SEACA.

Ford, Michele. 2019. *From Migrant to Worker: Global Unions and Temporary Labor Migration in Asia*. Ithaca: ILR Press.

Ford, Michele and Lenore Lyons. 2006. 'The Borders within: Mobility and Enclosure in the Riau Islands'. *Asia Pacific Viewpoint* 47 (2): 257–71.

Ford, Michele and Lenore Lyons. 2009. 'Fluid Boundaries: Modernity, Nation and Identity in the Riau Islands'. In *Indonesia beyond the Water's Edge: Managing an Archipelagic State*, edited by Robert Cribb and Michele Ford, 196–212. Singapore: ISEAS.

Ford, Michele and Lenore Lyons. 2011. 'Travelling the Aspal Route: Grey Labour Migration through an Indonesian Border Town'. In *The State and Illegality in Indonesia*, edited by Edward Aspinall and Gerry van Klinken, 107–22. Leiden: KITLV.

Ford, Michele and Lenore Lyons. 2012a. 'Smuggling Cultures in the Indonesia–Singapore Borderlands'. In *Transnational Flows and Permissive Polities: Ethnographies of Human Mobilities in Asia*, edited by Barak Kalir and Malini Sur, 91–108. Amsterdam: Amsterdam University Press.

Ford, Michele and Lenore Lyons. 2012b. 'Counter-Trafficking and Migrant Labour Activism In Indonesia's Periphery'. In *Labour Migration and Human Trafficking in Southeast Asia: Critical Perspectives*, edited by Michele Ford, Willem van Schendel and Lenore Lyons, 75–94. London: Routledge.

Ford, Michele and Lenore Lyons. 2013. 'Outsourcing Border Security: NGO Involvement in the Monitoring, Processing and Assistance of Indonesian Nationals Returning Illegally by Sea'. *Contemporary Southeast Asia* 35: 215–34.

Ford, Michele, Lenore Lyons and Wayne Palmer. 2010. 'Stopping the Hordes: A Critical Account of the Labour Government's Regional Approach to the Management of Asylum Seekers'. *Local-Global* 8: 28–35.

Ford, Michele, Lenore Lyons and Willem van Schendel (eds.). 2012. 'Labour Migration and Human Trafficking: An Introduction'. In *Labour Migration and Human Trafficking in Southeast Asia: Critical Perspectives*, edited by Michele Ford, Lenore Lyons and Willem van Schendel, 1–22. London: Routledge.

Francis, Angus and Rowena Maguire. 2013. *Protection of Refugees and Displaced Persons in the Asia Pacific Region*. London: Routledge.

Gerstl, Alfred and Belinda Helmke. 2012. 'The Association of Southast Asian Nations (ASEAN) and Climate Change: A Threat to National, Regime, and Human Security'. In *Human Security: Securing East Asia's Future*, edited by Benny Guan, 135–56. New York: Springer.

Grewcock, Michael. 2018. 'Bordering on Denial: State Persecution, Border Controls and the Rohingya Refugee Crisis'. In *Media, Crime and Racism*, edited by Monish Bhatia, Scott Poynting and Waqas Tufail, 161–80. New York: Palgrave Macmillan.

Hall, Andy. 2012. *Myanmar and Migrant Workers: Briefing and Recommendations*. Bangkok: Mahidol Migration Center.

Hamid, Hazreena. 2021. Policing the Migrants in Times of Covid-19. *Academia Letters*, Article 2178.

Han, Kirsten. 2020. Singapore's New Covid-19 Cases Reveal the Country's Two Very Different Realities. *The Washington Post*. 16 April. www.washingtonpost.com/opinions/2020/04/16/singapores-new-covid-19-cases-reveal-countrys-two-very-different-realities/

Harkins, Benjamin. 2019. *Thailand Migration Report 2019*. Bangkok: United Nations Thematic Working Group on Migration in Thailand.

Hedman, Eva-Lotta. 2008. 'Refuge, Governmentality and Citizenship: Capturing "Illegal Migrants" in Malaysia and Thailand'. *Government and Opposition* 43 (2): 358–83.

Henry, Nicholas. 2018. *Asylum, Work, and Precarity: Bordering the Asia–Pacific*. New York: Palgrave Macmillan.

Hill, Elizabeth, Marian Baird and Michele Ford. 2017. 'Work/Care Regimes in the Asia–Pacific: A Conceptual Framework'. In *Women, Work and Care in the Asia–Pacific*, edited by Marian Baird, Michele Ford and Elizabeth Hill, 1–22. Abingdon: Routledge.

Hilsdon, Anne-Marie. 2000. 'The Contemplacion Fiasco: The Hanging of a Filipino Domestic Worker in Singapore'. In *Human Rights and Gender Politics: Asia–Pacific Perspectives*, edited by Anne-Marie Hilsdon, Martha MacIntyre, Vera Mackie and Maila Stivens, 167–87. London: Routledge.

Hochschild, Arlie. 2000. 'Global Care Chains and Emotional Surplus Value'. In *On the Edge: Living with Global Capitalism*, edited by Will Hutton and Anthony Giddens, 130–46. London: Jonathan Cape.

Hoffstaedter, Gerhard. 2014. 'Place-Making: Chin Refugees, Citizenship and the State in Malaysia'. *Citizenship Studies* 18 (8): 871–84.

Hoffstaedter, Gerhard. 2015. 'Urban Refugees and UNHCR in Kuala Lumpur: Dependency, Assistance and Survival'. In *Urban Refugees: Challenges in Protection, Services and Policy*, edited by Gerhard Hoffstaedter and Koichi Koizumi, 187–205. London: Routledge.

Hoffstaedter, Gerhard. 2017. 'Refugees, Islam, and the State: The Role of Religion in Providing Sanctuary in Malaysia'. *Journal of Immigrant & Refugee Studies* 15 (3): 287–304.

Horstmann, Alexander. 2004. *Incorporation and Resistance: Borderlands, Transnational Communities and Social Change in Southeast Asia*. Tokyo: Tokyo University of Foreign Studies.

Horstmann, Alexander and Reed Wadley. 2006. 'Introduction: Centering the Margin in Southeast Asia'. In *Centering the Margin: Agency and Narrative in Southeast Asian Borderlands*, edited by Alexander Horstmann and Reed Wadley, 1–24. Oxford: Berghahn.

HRW. 2015. *Thailand: Mass Graves of Rohingya Found in Trafficking Camp*. New York: Human Rights Watch.

HRW. 2018. *Hidden Chains: Rights Abuses and Forced Labor in Thailand's Fishing Industry*. New York: Human Rights Watch.

Huang, Shirlena and Brenda Yeoh. 1998. 'Ties That Bind: State Policy and Migrant Female Domestic Helpers in Singapore'. *Geoforum* 27 (4): 479–93.

Hugo, Graeme, George Tan and Caven Napitupulu. 2014. *Indonesia as a Transit Country in Irregular Migration to Australia*. Canberra: Department of Immigration and Border Protection.

ILO. 2010. *International Labour Migration: A Rights-Based Approach*. Geneva: ILO.

ILO. 2015. *Review of the Effectiveness of the MOUs in Managing Labour Migration between Thailand and Neighbouring Countries*. Bangkok: ILO.

ILO. 2017. *Building Labour Migration Policy Coherence in Myanmar*. Yangon: ILO.

ILO. 2019a. *Public Attitudes towards Migrant Workers in Japan, Malaysia, Singapore and Thailand*. Bangkok: ILO.

ILO. 2019b. *TRIANGLE in ASEAN Quarterly Briefing Note: Malaysia*. Bangkok: ILO.

ILO. 2020a. *Covid-19: Impact on Migrant Workers and Country Response in Thailand*. Bangkok: ILO.

ILO. 2020b. *TRIANGLE in ASEAN Quarterly Briefing Note: Thailand*. Bangkok: ILO.

IMF. 2008. *Lao People's Democratic Republic: Second Poverty Reduction Strategy Paper*. Washington, DC: IMF.

Immigration Department of Malaysia. 2020a. 'Foreign Domestic Helper (FDH)'. Accessed 8 June. www.imi.gov.my/portal2017/index.php/en/foreign-domestic-helper-fdh.html.

Immigration Department of Malaysia. 2020b. 'Recruitment Terms and Conditions of Foreign Workers'. Accessed 8 June. www.imi.gov.my/portal2017/index.php/en/foreign-worker.html.

IOM. 2003. *Labour Migration: Trends, Challenges and Policy Responses in Countries of Origin*. Geneva: IOM.

IOM. 2019. *World Migration Report 2020*. Geneva: IOM.

Jongwilaiwan, Rattana and Eric Thompson. 2013. 'Thai Wives in Singapore and Transnational Patriarchy'. *Gender, Place & Culture* 20 (3): 363–81.

Kassim, Azizah. 2009. 'Filipino Refugees in Sabah: State Responses, Public Stereotypes and the Dilemma over Their Future'. *Japanese Journal of Southeast Asian Studies* 47 (1): 52–88.

Kaur, Amarjit. 2014. 'Managing Labour Migration in Malaysia: Guest Worker Programs and the Regularisation of Irregular Labour Migrants as a Policy Instrument'. *Asian Studies Review* 38 (3): 345–66.

Killias, Olivia. 2014. 'Intimate Encounters: The Ambiguities of Belonging in the Transnational Migration of Indonesian Domestic Workers to Malaysia'. *Citizenship Studies* 18 (8): 885–99.

Lam, Theodora and Brenda Yeoh. 2018. "Migrant Mothers, Left-behind Fathers: The Negotiation of Gender Subjectivities in Indonesia and the Philippines'. *Gender, Place and Culture* 25 (1): 104–17.

Lam, Tom. 2000. 'The Exodus of Hoa Refugees from Vietnam and Their Settlement in Guangxi: China's Refugee Settlement Strategies'. *Journal of Refugee Studies* 13 (4): 374–90.

Leng, Cheng Heng, Brenda Yeoh and Rashidah Shuib. 2012. 'Circuitous Pathways: Marriage as a Route toward (Il) Legality for Indonesian Migrant Workers in Malaysia'. *Asian and Pacific Migration Journal* 21(3): 317–44.

Lewa, Chris. 2008. 'Asia's New Boat People'. *Forced Migration Review* 30: 40–1.

Lindio-McGovern, Ligaya. 2017. 'The Philippines: Pressures for Change in the Work/Care Regime'. In *Women, Work and Care in the Asia-Pacific*, edited by Marian Baird, Michele Ford and Elizabeth Hill, 87–101. Abingdon: Routledge.

Lindquist, Johan. 2010. 'Images and Evidence: Human Trafficking, Auditing, and the Production of Illicit Markets in Southeast Asia and beyond'. *Public Culture* 22 (2): 223–36.

Locher-Scholten, Elsbeth. 2004. *Sumatran Sultanate and Colonial State: Jambi and the Rise of Dutch Imperialism, 1830–1907*. Ithaca: Cornell Southeast Asia.

Lumayag, Linda. 2016. 'Marriage "During" Work Migration: Lived Experiences of Filipinos Marriage Migrants in Malaysia'. In *Marriage Migration in Asia: Emerging Minorities at the Frontiers of Nation-States*, edited by Sarii Ishii, 73–104. Singapore: NUS Press.

Lyons, Lenore. 2017. 'Singapore: Contradictions in the Work/Care Regime'. In *Women, Work and Care in the Asia-Pacific*, edited by Marian Baird, Michele Ford and Elizabeth Hill, 55–70. Abingdon: Routledge.

Lyons, Lenore and Michele Ford. 2008. 'Love, Sex and the Spaces In-between: Kepri Wives and Their Cross-Border Husbands'. *Citizenship Studies* 12 (1): 55–72.

Lyons, Lenore and Michele Ford. 2010. '"Where Are Your Victims?": How Sexual Health Advocacy Came to Be Counter-Trafficking in Indonesia's Riau Islands. *International Feminist Journal of Politics* 12(2): 255–64.

Lyons, Lenore and Michele Ford. 2014. 'Trafficking Versus Smuggling: Malaysia's Anti-Trafficking in Persons Act'. In *Human Trafficking in Asia: Forcing Issues*, edited by Sallie Yea, 35–48. London: Routledge.

Mahanty, Sango. 2022. *Unsettled Frontiers: Market Formation in the Cambodia–Vietnam Borderlands*. Ithaca: Cornell University Press.

Manpower Research and Statistics Department. 2020. *Labour Force in Singapore*. Singapore: Ministry of Manpower.

McAdam, Jane. 2012. *Climate Change, Forced Migration and International Law*. Oxford: Oxford University Press.

McAdam, Marika. 2018. 'The Antics of Semantics in International Law'. *Anti-Trafficking Review* 11: 125–8.

McConnahie, Kirsten. 2014. 'Forced Migration in South-East Asia and East Asia'. In *The Oxford Handbook of Refugee and Forced Migration Studies*, edited by Elena Fiddian-Qasmiyeh, Gil Loescher, Katy Long and Nando Sigona, 626–39. Oxford: Oxford University Press.

McDowell, Christopher and Marita Eastmond. 2002. 'Transitions, State Building and the "Residual" Refugee Problem: East Timor and Cambodian Repatriation Experience'. *Australian Journal of Human Rights* 8 (1): 7–29.

McKeown, Adam. 2012. 'How the Box Became Black: Brokers and the Creation of the Free Migrant'. *Pacific Affairs* 85 (1): 21–45.

Meyer, Claus and Sebastian Boll. 2018. 'Categorising Migrants: Standards, Complexities, and Politics'. *Anti-trafficking Review* 18: 1–14.

Millock, Katrin. 2015. 'Migration and Environment'. *Annual Review of Resource Economics* 7(1): 35–60.

Missbach, Antje. 2012. *Separatist Conflict in Indonesia the Long-Distance Politics of the Acehnese Diaspora*. London: Routledge.

Missbach, Antje. 2018. 'Big Fears about Small Boats: How Asylum Seekers Keep Upsetting the Indonesia–Australia Relationship'. In *Strangers Next Door? Indonesia and Australia in the Asian Century*, edited by Timothy Lindsey and Dave McRae, 125–48. Oxford: Hart.

Molland, Sverre. 2012. 'The Inexorable Quest for Trafficking Hotspots along Thai–Lao Border'. In *Labour Migration and Human Trafficking in Southeast Asia: Critical Perspectives*, edited by Michele Ford, Lenore Lyons and Willem van Schendel, 57–74. London: Routledge.

Moretti, Sebastien. 2015. 'The Challenge of Durable Solutions for Refugees at the Thai–Myanmar Border'. *Refugee Survey Quarterly* 34: 70–94.

Morris-Suzuki, Tessa. 2006. 'Changing Border Control Regimes and Their Impact on Migration in Asia'. In *Mobility, Labour Migration and Border Controls in Asia*, edited by Amarjit Kaur and Ian Metcalfe, 8–22. New York: Palgrave Macmillan

Murugasu, Sheila. 2017. *The State and the Transnational Politics of Migrants: A Study of the Chins and the Acehnese in Malaysia*. London: Palgrave Macmillan.

Mutaqin, Zezen. 2018. 'The Rohingya Refugee Crisis and Human Rights: What Should ASEAN Do?'. *Asia–Pacific Journal on Human Rights and the Law* 19 (1): 1–26.

Natali, Claudia, Euan McDougall, Sally Stubbington and Jerrold Huguet. 2014. 'International Migration Policy in Thailand'. In *Thailand Migration Report 2014*, edited by Jerrold Huguet, 13–26. Bangkok: International Organization for Migration.

Neo, Jaclyn. 2015. 'Riots and Rights: Law and Exclusion in Singapore's Migrant Worker Regime'. *Asian Journal of Law and Society* 2 (1): 137–68.

Ng, Chin-Keong. 1976. *The Chinese in Riau: A Community on an Unstable and Restrictive Frontier*. Singapore: Institute of Humanities and Social Sciences, Nanyang University.

Nurchayati. 2017. 'Sociocultural Change and the Life Cycle: A Study of Javanese Village Women's Decisions on Transnational Labour Migration and Their Impact'. PhD Thesis, The University of Sydney.

Obokata, Reiko, Veronis, Luisa and McLeman, Robert 2014. 'Empirical Research on International Environmental Migration: A Systematic Review'. *Population and Environment* 36: 111–35.

Offord, Baden. 2013. 'Queer Activist Intersections in Southeast Asia: Human Rights and Cultural Studies'. *Asian Studies Review* 37 (3): 335–49.

OHCHR. 2002. *Recommended Principles and Guidelines on Human Rights and Human Trafficking*. Geneva: OHCHR.

Okudaira, Akiko and Hitoshi Nasu. 2013. 'Revisiting the Conception of Protection in International Refugee Law: Implications of the Protracted Refugee Situation on the Thai–Myanmar Border'. In *Protection of Refugees and Displaced Persons in the Asia Pacific Region*, edited by Angus Francis and Rowena Maguire, 171–83. Farnham: Ashgate.

Ong, Yanchun. 2014. 'Singapore's Phantom Workers'. *Journal of Contemporary Asia* 44 (3): 443–63.

Osborne, Milton. 1980. 'The Indochinese Refugees: Cause and Effects'. *International Affairs* 56 (1): 37–53.

Palmer, Wayne. 2016. *Indonesia's Overseas Labour Migration Programme, 1969–2010*. Leiden: Brill.

Palupi, Sri and Najib Yasser. 2002. 'Laporan Investigasi Buruh Migran Indonesia (TKI) di Nunukan: Korban Praktek Perbudakan Terselubung Indonesia – Malaysia'. Unpublished report. Jakarta: Jaringan Relawan Kemanusiaan untuk Nunukan.

Parreñas, Rhacel. 2005. *Children of Global Migration: Transnational Families and Gendered Woes*. Stanford: Stanford University Press.

Pidd, Helen. 2019. 'Home Office Gives Man Asylum after Accepting People Can Be Gay and Single'. *The Guardian*, 24 December. www.theguardian.com/uk-news/2019/dec/23/home-office-gives-man-asylum-after-accepting-people-can-be-gay-and-single.

Piper, Nicola. 2006. 'Gendering the Politics of Migration'. *International Migration Review* 40: 133–64.

Prabandari, Atin and Yunizar Adiputera. 2019. 'Alternative Paths to Refugee and Asylum Seeker Protection in Malaysia and Indonesia'. *Asian and Pacific Migration Journal* 28 (2): 132–54.

Purdey, Jemma. 2005. *Anti-Chinese Violence in Indonesia, 1996–1999*. Singapore: NUS Press.

Renshaw, Catherine. 2019. 'Myanmar's Transition without Justice'. *Journal of Current Southeast Asian Affairs* 38 (3): 381–403.

Resink, Gertrudes. 1968. *Indonesia's History between the Myths: Essays in Legal History and Historical Theory*. The Hague: Van Hoeve.

Richardson, Liam and Rachael Pettigrew. 2022. 'Migrant Agricultural Workers: A Comparative Analysis of Both Policy and COVID-19 Response in Thailand, Italy, and Canada'. *SN Social Sciences* 2 (11): 236–63.

Rodriguez, Robyn. 2010. *Migrants for Export: How the Philippines State Brokers Labor to the World*. Minneapolis: Minnesota University Press.

Rungmanee, Soimart. 2016. 'Illegal but Licit: Migrant Mobility and the Negotiation of Legality in the Northeast Thai–Lao Borderlands'. *Asia Pacific Viewpoint* 57 (2): 221–31.

Sandy, Larissa. 2012. 'International Politics, Anti-trafficking Measures and Sex Work in Cambodia'. In *Labour Migration and Human Trafficking in Southeast Asia: Critical Perspectives*, edited by Michele Ford, Lenore Lyons and Willem van Schendel, 41–56. London: Routledge.

Schober, Juliane. 1995. 'The Theravāda Buddhist Engagement with Modernity in Southeast Asia: Whither the Social Paradigm of the Galactic Polity?'. *Journal of Southeast Asian Studies* 26(2): 307–25.

Shamir, Hila. 2012. 'A Labor Paradigm for Human Trafficking'. *UCLA Law Review* 60 (1): 76–136.

Sheldrick, Drew. 2016. 'Gay Malaysian Student Granted Refugee Status'. *SBS*, 7 April. www.sbs.com.au/topics/pride/article/2016/04/07/gay-malaysian-student-granted-refugee-status.

Siddique, Sharon. 1981. 'Some Aspects of Malay-Muslim Ethnicity in Peninsular Malaysia'. *Contemporary Southeast Asia* 3 (1): 76–87.

Singapore Government. 2012. *Employment of Foreign Manpower Act (Version in Force from 1 April 2019)*. Singapore: Ministry of Manpower.

South, Ashley. 2008. *Ethnic Politics in Burma: States of Conflict*. London: Routledge.

Stuart-Fox, Martin. 1997. *A History of Laos*. New York: Cambridge University Press.

Tagliacozzo, Eric. 2007. *Secret Trades, Porous Borders: Smuggling and States along a Southeast Asian Frontier, 1865–1915*. Singapore: National University of Singapore Press.

Tambiah, Stanley. 1977. 'The Galactic Polity: The Structure of Traditional Kingdoms in Southeast Asia'. *Annals of the New York Academy of Sciences* 293: 69–97.

Tambiah, Stanley. 1985. *Culture, Thought and Social Action: An Anthropological Perspective*. Cambridge, MA: Harvard University Press.

Tan, Nikolas. 2016. 'The Status of Asylum Seekers and Refugees in Indonesia'. *International Journal of Refugee Law* 28 (3): 365–83.

Taylor, Jessie. 2009. Behind Australian Doors: Examining the Conditions of Detention of Asylum Seekers in Indonesia. Accessed 3 November 2009. www.safecom.org.au/pdfs/behind-australian-doors-examining-the-conditions.pdf.

Tetenyi, Andras, Tamas Barczikay and Balazs Szent-Ivanyi. 2018. 'Refugees, Not Economic Migrants: Why Do Asylum-Seekers Register in Hungary?' *International Migration* 57 (5): 323–40.

UNHCR. 2020a. 'Climate Change and Disaster Displacement'. Accessed 22 July. www.unhcr.org/climate-change-and-disasters.html.

UNHCR. 2020b. 'Figures at a Glance in Malaysia'. Accessed 4 June. www.unhcr.org/figures-at-a-glance-in-malaysia.html.

UNHCR Indonesia. 2020. *Monthly Statistical Report*. Jakarta: UNHCR Indonesia.

UNHCR Statistics. 2020. 'The World in Numbers'. Accessed 4 June. http://popstats.unhcr.org/en/overview#_ga=2.107179394.1220598045.1591230072-1524251559.1590962897.

UNHRC. 2018. *Report of the Independent International Fact-Finding Mission on Myanmar*. Geneva: UNHRC.

UNHRC. 2019. *Detailed Findings of the Independent International Fact-Finding Mission on Myanmar*. Geneva: UNHRC.

UNODC. 2000. 'United Nations Convention against Transnational Organized Crime and the Protocols Thereto'. Accessed 30 June. www.unodc.org/unodc/en/organized-crime/intro/UNTOC.html.

UNODC. 2017. T*rafficking in Persons from Cambodia, Lao PDR and Myanmar to Thailand*. Bangkok: UNODC.

US Department of State. 2019. *Trafficking in Persons Report*. Washington, DC: US Department of State.

van der Kroef, Justus. 1958. 'On the Writing of Indonesian History'. *Pacific Affairs* 31 (4): 3352–71.

van Schendel, Willem. 2005. 'Spaces of Engagement: How Borderlands, Illicit Flows, and Territorial States Interlock'. In *Illicit Flows and Criminal Things: States, Borders, and the Other Side of Globalization*, edited by Willem van Schendel and Itty Abraham, 38–68. Bloomington: Indiana University Press.

Vang, Chia Youyee. 2016. 'Children of Hmong Refugees from Laos: Transnational Lives and the Politics of Negotiating Place'. In *Southeast Asian Migration: People on the Move in Search of Work, Refuge, and Belonging*, edited by Khatharya Um and Sofia Gaspar, 137–58. Brighton: Sussex Academic Press.

Varagur, Krithika. 2019. 'Indonesia's Queer Panic'. *LRB Blog*, 17 April. www.lrb.co.uk/blog/2019/april/indonesia-s-queer-panic.

von der Borch, Rosslyn. 2008. 'Straddling Worlds: Indonesian Migrant Domestic Workers in Singapore'. In *Women and Work in Indonesia*, edited by Michele Ford and Lyn Parker, 195–214. London: Routledge.

Voss, Loren. 2018. 'Choosing Words with Purpose: Framing Immigration and Refugee Issues as National Security Threats to Avoid Issues of Social Policy'. *Yale Journal of International Affairs* 13: 39–52.

Wake, Caitlin. 2016. *'Turning a Blind Eye': The Policy Response to Rohingya Refugees in Malaysia*. London: Overseas Development Institute.

Wake, Caitlin and Tania Cheung. 2016. *Livelihood Strategies of Rohingya Refugees in Malaysia: 'We Want to Live in Dignity'*. London: Overseas Development Institute.

Wennerstein, John and Denise Robbins. 2017. *Rising Tides: Climate Refugees in the Twenty-First Century*. Bloomington: Indiana University Press.

West, Brad. 2008. 'Collective Memory and Crisis: The 2002 Bali Bombing, National Heroic Archetypes and the Counter-narrative of Cosmopolitan Nationalism'. *Journal of Sociology* 44 (4): 337–53.

Wijaya, Hendri and Sharyn Davies. 2019. 'The Unfulfilled Promise of Democracy: Lesbian and Gay Activism in Indonesia'. In *Activists in Transition: Progressive Politics in Democratic Indonesia*, edited by Thushara Dibley and Michele Ford, 153–70. Ithaca: Cornell University Press.

Winarnita, Monika, Carol Chan and Leslie Butt. 2020. 'Narratives of Exile Twenty Years On: Long-term Impacts of Indonesia's 1998 Violence on Transnational Chinese-Indonesian Women'. *Identities* 27: 191–209.

Winichakul, Thongchai. 1994. *Siam Mapped: A History of the Geo-Body of a Nation*. Honolulu: University of Hawai'i Press.

Wise, Amanda. 2006. *Exile and Return among the East Timorese*. Philadelphia: University of Pennsylvania Press.

Wolters, Oliver. 1968. 'Ayudhyā and the Rearward Part of the World'. *Journal of the Royal Asiatic Society* 100 (2): 166–78.

Wong, Diana and Teuku Afrizal Anwar. 2003. 'Migran Gelap: Indonesian Migrants in Malaysia's Irregular Labour Economy'. In *Unauthorized Migration in Southeast Asia*, edited by Graziano Battistella and Maruja Asis, 169–227. Quezon City: Scalabrini Migration Center.

Wong, Lester and Tee Zhuo. 2020. Record 120 New Coronavirus cases in Singapore, 2 Foreign Worker Dormitories Gazetted as Isolation Areas. *The Straits Times*. 14 April. www.straitstimes.com/singapore/coronavirus-record-120-new-covid-19-cases-in-spore-two-foreign-worker-dormitories-gazetted.

Wong, Mee-Lian Roy Chan, Hiok Hee Tan et al. 2012. 'Sex Work and Risky Sexual Behaviors among Foreign Entertainment Workers in Urban Singapore: Findings from Mystery Client Survey'. *Journal of Urban Health* 89 (6): 1031–44.

World Bank. 2007. *Kompleksitas Mechanisme Penempatan BMP ke Luar Negeri: Beberapa Permasalahan dan Alternatif Solusinya*. Jakarta: World Bank.

World Bank. 2017. *Forcibly Displaced: Toward a Development Approach Supporting Refugees, the Internally Displaced, and Their Hosts*. Washington, DC: World Bank.

World Bank. 2020a. 'East Asia & Pacific'. Accessed 24 July. https://data.worldbank.org/region/east-asia-and-pacific.

World Bank. 2020b. 'GDP Per Capita (Current US$)'. Accessed 24 July. https://data.worldbank.org/indicator/NY.GDP.PCAP.CD?end=2018&start=1960.

Yea, Sallie. 2015. 'Trafficked Enough? Missing Bodies, Migrant Labour Exploitation, and the Classification of Trafficking Victims in Singapore'. *Antipode* 47 (4): 1080–100.

Yeoh, Brenda, Shirlena Huang and Joaquin Gonzalez. 1999. 'Migrant Female Domestic Workers: Debating the Economic, Social and Political Impacts in Singapore'. *International Migration Review* 33 (1): 114–36.

Yusuf, Imtiyaz. 2007. 'The Southern Thailand Conflict and the Muslim World'. *Journal of Muslim Minority Affairs* 27 (2): 319–39.

Zarni, Maung and Alice Cowley. 2014. 'The Slow-Burning Genocide of Myanmar's Rohingya'. *Pacific Rim Law and Policy Journal* 23 (3): 683–754.

Zetter, Roger. 2010. 'Protecting People Displaced by Climate Change: Some Conceptual Challenges'. In *Climate Change and Displacement: Multidisciplinary Perspectives*, edited by Jane McAdam, 131–50. London: Hart.

Zhang, Juan. 2012. 'A Trafficking "Not-Spot" in a China–Vietnam Border Town'. In *Labour Migration and Human Trafficking in Southeast Asia: Critical Perspectives*, edited by Michele Ford, Lyons Lenore and Willem van Schendel, 95–111. London: Routledge.

Zhang, Juan and Brenda Yeoh. 2020. 'Searching for Oriental Simplicity: Foreign Brides and the Asian Family in Singapore'. *Gender, Place & Culture* 27 (10): 1415–37.

Zimmermann, Susan. 2011. 'Reconsidering the Problem of "Bogus" Refugees with "Socio-economic Motivations" for Seeking Asylum'. *Mobilities* 6 (3): 335–52.

Acknowledgements

This Element reflects work I have done alone and with others over the twenty years since I finished my PhD in 2003. My interest in labour migration was sparked by debates in the early 2000s about whether trade unions could be convinced to take migrants seriously, or whether migrant labour advocacy would remain entirely within the NGO world. Quite separately, but most fittingly, I started thinking about bordering and borderlands as a student – an interest entirely separate to my PhD work – when Edward Aspinall, a co-editor of this series, asked me if I would like to give a paper at the 2002 Indonesia Update at the Australian National University. Too good to refuse, this invitation prompted an initial exploration of identity and separatist sentiment in Mainland Riau and the Riau Islands.

These interests came together when I began working with my long-term collaborator, Lenore Lyons. While our conversations initially focused on labour migration from Indonesia to Singapore, we soon settled on the much richer topic of life in the Singapore–Indonesia borderlands. We both remained interested in international labour migration, but increasingly focused also on border-crossers of other kinds. For many years, we researched and wrote on everything from bordering practices, to smuggling and to sex tourism. It was a heady time to be thinking about these issues with the growing emphasis on the prevention of human trafficking in the US and elsewhere and its reverberations through Southeast Asia.

After a decade or so of working together on this and related projects, Lenore made the difficult decision to leave academia. We continued to collaborate for some years on various publications, and remain close friends. In the meantime, I began working on other projects including a large study of union and NGO responses to labour migration in East and Southeast Asian destination countries. While I have continued to consider bordering and border-crossing in my more recent work on transnational labour activism – undertaken mostly in collaboration with Michael Gillan – it is these earlier academic projects upon which this short book draws most.

I would also like to acknowledge the support provided by the Australian Research Council (ARC) for these (and later) projects. The borderlands study, ‘In the Shadow of Singapore: The Limits of Transnationalism in Insular Riau’ (DP0557368), was funded in 2005 through the Discovery Project scheme. My broader labour migration work was supported by another ARC grant, ‘From Migrant to Worker: New Transnational Responses to Temporary Labour

Migration in East and Southeast Asia' (DP080081). This work also benefitted from several smaller grants including a University of Wollongong Small Grant for a project on migrant labour in Singapore, an ARC International Linkage Grant for collaboration on comparative border studies (LX0882882), and an Australian-Netherlands Research Collaboration Workshop Grant (co-held with Willem van Schendel), which led to an edited volume on labour migration and human trafficking, the contributions to which also influenced my thinking on bordering processes.

Finally, and as always, I want to thank my partner, Muliawarman, for his unfailing support over the last 30 or so years. When we met at university in Yogyakarta, we certainly had no idea where life would take us, but he has always been happy to come along for the ride. Engaging with Mul's extended family has very much shaped my experience and understanding of Indonesia. The link with this particular body of research is even more direct: the fact Mul was born in Tanjung Pinang, and that we have family there to this day, sparked and has very much sustained my interest in borderlands and the people who inhabit them and cross through them.

Cambridge Elements

Politics and Society in Southeast Asia

About the Series

The Elements series Politics and Society in Southeast Asia includes both country-specific and thematic studies on one of the world's most dynamic regions. Each title, written by a leading scholar of that country or theme, combines a succinct, comprehensive, up-to-date overview of debates in the scholarly literature with original analysis and a clear argument.

Cambridge Elements

Politics and Society in Southeast Asia

Elements in the Series

The Rise of Sophisticated Authoritarianism in Southeast Asia
Lee Morgenbesser

Rural Development in Southeast Asia
Jonathan Rigg

Fighting Armed Conflicts in Southeast Asia
Shane Joshua Barter

Democratic Deconsolidation in Southeast Asia
Marcus Mietzner

Islam and Political Power in Indonesia and Malaysia
Joseph Chinyong Liow

Civil Society in Southeast Asia
Garry Rodan

The Meaning of Democracy in Southeast Asia: Liberalism, Egalitarianism and Participation
Diego Fossati and Ferran Martinez i Coma

Organized Labor in Southeast Asia
Teri L. Caraway

The Philippines: From "People Power" to Democratic Backsliding
Mark R. Thompson

Contesting Social Welfare in Southeast Asia
Andrew Rosser and John Murphy

Myanmar
Nick Cheesman

The Politics of Cross-Border Mobility in Southeast Asia
Michele Ford

A full series listing is available at: www.cambridge.org/ESEA

For EU product safety concerns, contact us at Calle de José Abascal, 56–1°, 28003 Madrid, Spain or eugpsr@cambridge.org.

www.ingramcontent.com/pod-product-compliance
Ingram Content Group UK Ltd.
Pitfield, Milton Keynes, MK11 3LW, UK
UKHW022143080726
473066UK00010B/723

* 9 7 8 1 1 0 8 7 2 2 8 9 6 *